TO HAVE & TO HOLD

PREPARING FOR A GODLY MARRIAGE

BYRON & CARLA
WEATHERSBEE

LifeWay Press® Nashville, Tennessee

Published by LifeWay Press® • ©2017 Byron and Carla Weathersbee • Reprinted February 2019

ISBN 978-1-4300-6355-1
Item 005791139
Dewey decimal classification: 306.81
Subject heading: MARRIAGE \ DOMESTIC RELATIONS \ MARRIAGE COUNSELING

To order additional copies of this resource, write LifeWay Church Resources Customer Service; One LifeWay Plaza; Nashville, TN 37234-0113; FAX order to 615.251.5933; call toll-free 800.458.2772; email orderentry@lifeway.com; order online at LifeWay.com; or visit the LifeWay Christian Store serving you.

Printed in the United States of America.
Adult Ministry Publishing, LifeWay Church Resources,
One LifeWay Plaza, Nashville, TN 37234-0152

CONTENTS

DR. BYRON *and* CARLA WEATHERSBEE

Byron and Carla Weathersbee serve as the Executive Directors of Summers Mill Retreat and Conference Center in Salado, Texas. In addition, they lead Legacy Family Ministries, a ministry they co-founded in 1995. Legacy's mission is to pass on biblical principles from one generation to the next by providing marriage preparation for pre-engaged and engaged couples. Byron and Carla authored *Before Forever: How do you know that you know?*—a book for seriously dating couples.

Carla currently leads the women's ministry at their church, and Byron serves as an Elder. Byron has served on church staff, as a university chaplain, and recently as the vice president for student life at the University of Mary Hardin-Baylor.

Both Byron and Carla are graduates of Baylor University. Carla has done graduate work in exercise physiology and Byron earned his doctoral degree in leadership from The Southern Baptist Theological Seminary and a Master's degree from Southwestern Baptist Theological Seminary.

Carla and Byron live in Salado, Texas, and have been married for over thirty years. They have three grown children. Recently, two of their children were married.

INTRODUCTION TO THE VOWS:

GETTING STARTED

> "I'll go anywhere with God, as long as it is forward."[1]
> **DAVID LIVINGSTONE**

WHAT IS THE PROPER AGE TO GET MARRIED?

Isabella, an eight-year-old, says, "Eighty-four! Because at that age, you don't have to work anymore, and you can spend all your time loving each other in your bedroom."

Five-year-old Jacob had a different perspective. He thinks, "Once I'm done with kindergarten, I'm going to find me a wife."

For us it was somewhere between kindergarten and age eighty-four. We met as college students and dated for a year and a half before I asked her the big question—"Will you marry me?"

There is no question that I invested more energy in buying her ring and planning the proposal than I ever did preparing for the marriage itself. Carla spent countless hours picking out her dress, organizing the wedding, and making sure everyone was pleased with her decisions. We spent a whopping one hour in premarital counseling with our minister, a month prior to our wedding day. In that hour, we spent thirty minutes on the details of the wedding ceremony, ten minutes on finances, ten minutes on in-laws, and ten minutes on sex. To this day, I can only remember ten minutes of our time together that last day—the last ten minutes.

As you begin the countdown toward your wedding day, we hope you will spend these days not only preparing for the perfect big day, but that you will also invest time and energy into building a healthy, lifelong marriage. In the days ahead you will need to be empowered by something greater than yourselves—or Someone. When you do not have enough power or ability to love your mate in your own capacity, God will enable you to love. We have a Savior who gives life, hope, and purpose. As you prepare for your marriage, make time in your calendar to develop your spiritual foundation as individuals and as a couple while you grow in your understanding of Jesus Christ and make family a priority. Allow Him to be your teacher, instructor, guide, counselor, and coach as you discover biblical principles that govern the way life can be lived to the fullest.

To Have and To Hold offers a different approach to premarital counseling. Instead, we like to think of it as marriage education. We feel that through preventive education couples can be equipped to avoid divorce and to build strong marriages and healthy families. In preparing this course, we have taken into account your busy schedules, the importance of interaction, and the need for a simplified lifestyle during your engagement.

BUSY SCHEDULES

The days prior to a wedding can be hectic. Many couples make the mistake of collecting great resources and then becoming overwhelmed by the amount of information they've gathered. Oftentimes the resources are placed on a shelf only to be retrieved during a major crisis several years later—often too little, too late—when the damage is already done.

To Have and To Hold takes advantage of your leisure time—whatever time is left when you are not sleeping, eating, working, going to school, or planning a wedding. Of course, you will need discipline to maximize the impact of *To Have and To Hold*, but we have created weekly activities that allow you to capitalize on your time together as a couple. You will make time for each other, so why not use the time positively to work through some of the issues vital to a healthy, lifelong relationship? Some of the weekly assignments are designed to be fun, creative, and light. Remember, it is okay to relax, laugh, and escape from the wedding plans. Finding a balanced approach will help you gain insight during the fast-paced days before you.

INTERACTIVE

Each week you will be given four learning activities that coincide with the week's topic. You may be encouraged to meditate on a Scripture passage, do a biblical word study, go to a romantic place, or complete some other activity that creatively challenges your thinking. These assignments are not a major time commitment, but they are vital as you work through issues. Our ultimate goal in *To Have and To Hold* is for the two of you to interact, discuss, and possibly debate the subject matter. We believe it is better for you to discuss your thoughts, ideals, fears, and questions rather than simply read the latest resource regarding that issue. We encourage you to color outside the lines and creatively adapt each session to meet your needs as you work through the Bible study book. Remember, the keys are interaction and communication as you seek God's principles for a fulfilling marriage.

PRACTICAL AND SIMPLE

Not many people enjoy reading long, involved, and complicated technical manuals. Thus, our attempt to challenge your thinking is simple and practical. This Bible study book is not intended to be a comprehensive, in-depth, "all-answer" resource. Instead, we hope to equip you with some basic tools that are as old as time. Oftentimes simplistic principles are easy to understand but complicated to live out. Hopefully, as you work through each section, your teacher, the Holy Spirit, will help you find practical ways to implement the biblical principles we present. As you build a biblical foundation, it is important to begin with the basics and then add on what you know. The focus of *To Have and To Hold* is life change—practical and simple life change.

GETTING STARTED

Before you get started, you will need to understand a few more things regarding the *To Have and To Hold* Bible study book.

As you will notice, most sections of the study parallel part of the traditional marriage vows and the study concludes with keys to living out those vows. Each session has been designed for you to work through as a couple and then to meet with a pastor, mentor, or small group of other engaged couples to gain encouragement, share insight, and debate opinions. The focus is not on the Bible study book or teacher but on the learning process that God is bringing to your lives.

If you would like to do further study on a topic or dig deeper, our website, LifeWay.com/ToHaveAndToHold, provides helpful and comprehensive resources.

As the wedding countdown begins for you, we hope marriage will be as rewarding and fulfilling for you as it has been for us. To be honest, it is the hardest thing we have ever done. The old cliché of "Anything worth having is worth working for!" really does ring true here.[2]

During the next several weeks, work hard, invest much, be real, and be honest. The return on your investment will be huge. As you meet at the altar, may your wedding day fulfill your dreams; but more importantly, may you be adequately prepared to fulfill your vows—and enjoy the process. Have fun! The *best* is yet to come!

Byron & Carla

Byron and Carla Weathersbee

THE PURPOSE *for* MARRIAGE

WHY AM I GETTING MARRIED?

OVERVIEW

The purpose of this section is to help you understand the biblical foundation for marriage. Marriage is an earthly picture of a divine institution. Thus, your marriage has the potential to glorify God and to provide an example to the world of what God's home will be like. Our hope is for you to establish a firm spiritual foundation upon which to build your lives and your marriage.

> *"A good marriage is not finding the right person so much as it is being the right person."*[1]
> **STEPHEN CROTTS**

"I TAKE THEE TO BE MY WEDDED WIFE/HUSBAND"

> "... they are no longer two, but one."
> **MATTHEW 19:6**

I (Carla) will never forget the feeling of watching my last bridesmaid walk down the aisle, leaving only me and my dad. The moment I had anticipated for a lifetime was finally here. I wanted our wedding to be more than a mere formality. I wanted to soak in every moment and every detail. My dad was silent and calm as usual. Yet I could sense how proud and happy he was to present me to the man with whom I was to spend the rest of my life.

When my dad placed my hand in Byron's hand, calmness and assurance replaced my anxiety. I knew without a doubt that this moment was right. I had never been so sure of a decision in all my life. That hot summer day, we began the process of two becoming one. I took Byron to become part of me—all of me.

LIVING OUT THE VOWS

Three children (one of which had childhood cancer), twelve moves in five cities, and thirty plus years of ministry later, I now realize how crucial it is to grasp God's purpose and plan for marriage. During our engagement, my expectations of marriage reflected reasonable and God-given desires. I wanted companionship, affection, and someone with whom to share life. However, oftentimes my motives for pursuing these desires were self-centered. Unfortunately, too many couples enter marriage with a consumer mentality, each person focusing on his or her own happiness rather than that of his or her partner. We are, instead, to enter into a loving covenant, considering the other as more important than self.

UNDERSTANDING THE PURPOSE

Most engaged couples come to their wedding days with hopes of a satisfying companionship. Why, then, do many newlyweds lose hope and allow isolation to replace oneness? Neither spouse feels loved, respected, or understood. Boredom replaces romance. Wonder turns to a wandering relationship. One thing I have learned: good marriages require work, commitment, and laughter.

As your journey begins, our desire is to help you establish a firm spiritual foundation. Take the time to prepare by working through the questions behind the question, "Why am I getting married?"

Faithful Guide,

You are the Creator God, so I am not going to attempt to stretch the truth—You know why I want to be married. You know I want it to be a good marriage. As I pursue what I want, I need You to lead me to do what I ought to do, keep me in check, and please keep my emotions from controlling my mind and spirit. Help each—mind, spirit, and emotion—to work in harmony. Teach me to be content with who I am but more importantly to understand You and Your purposes. Upon that realization, teach me deep truths about trust, love, and hope. I seek to know You and Your intention for marriage. I recognize that we pray in Jesus' name. Amen.

PREP WORK

ONE

List ten reasons why you want to be married.

1.

2.

3.

4.

5.

6.

7.

8.

9.

10.

List ten reasons why you feel you are ready for marriage.

1.

2.

3.

4.

5.

6.

7.

8.

9.

10.

TWO

Study the following Scripture passages and what they say about marriage.
    Genesis 2:18-25

Matthew 19:2-9

Mark 10:6-9

Ephesians 5:21-33

Hebrews 13:4-7

After reflecting on the verses above, in your opinion, what are some of God's purposes for marriage?

THREE

Go on a walk with your (future) spouse, make sure to choose one of your favorite places to walk. Take this opportunity to discuss your ideas, dreams, and fears about marriage. Complete Prep Work #3 and #4 together.

Consider the following questions to prompt your thinking:

What are you most excited about regarding your marriage?

In what ways are you and your partner similar? Different?

What fears do you have about marriage?

What have you learned this week about your readiness for marriage? How does all that match up with what you found in the Bible regarding God's purpose for marriage?

FOUR

After your walk together, attempt to come up with a concise definition of marriage. Write your definition below:

Marriage is ...

DRIVING QUESTIONS

WHAT DO YOU EXPECT TO GET OUT OF MARRIAGE?

What are some expectations you have for your marriage?

Our expectations often dictate our direction for marriage. How?

What needs do you hope are met?

What are some of God's expectations for marriage?

WHY ENTER A MARRIAGE COVENANT?

Read Genesis 2:15-25. What is Adam's dilemma?

What is God's solution?

What are some challenges to maintaining oneness?

How are a covenant and a contract similar? Different?

Covenant literally means "cutting [or] passing between pieces of flesh."[2] The Hebrew word picture was the joining of flesh, hearts being meshed, sacrifice being made.

"Too many couples enter marriage blinded by unrealistic expectations. They believe a high level of continuous romantic love should characterize the relationship. As one young adult said, 'I wanted marriage to fulfill all my desires. I needed security, someone to take care of me, intellectual stimulation, and economic security immediately—but it just wasn't like that!' People are looking for something 'magical' to happen in marriage. But magic doesn't make a marriage work: hard work does."[3]

H. NORMAN WRIGHT

WHY DOES DISILLUSIONMENT COME
WHEN THE HONEYMOON IS OVER?

Disillusionment is the gap between what is expected and reality. H. Norman Wright says, "I think that almost everyone who marries eventually experiences some degree of disillusionment ... it's usually an increased awareness that the relationship isn't going as well as expected."[4]

How does a newly married couple establish realistic expectations for the first few years of marriage?

What can a couple do to prepare for the disillusionment phase?

HOW CAN DISILLUSIONMENT LEAD TO
FULFILLMENT AND SATISFACTION?

How do we find freedom from the expectations of others?

In the margin, list a few ways to keep from losing hope and becoming discouraged during the disillusionment phase.

What can be learned from times when we let one another down?

SYNOPSIS

"Strong families hold the key to a strong society...because every other institution in society is predicated on and dependent upon strong families. And you can't have strong families without God as the centerpiece of the marriage union that ties that family together."[5]

DR. TONY EVANS

God's purposes for marriage are much higher and greater than our own. In Genesis 2:18, God said "It is not good for the man to be alone," and He created Eve as an answer to that aloneness. Even though Adam had a perfect relationship with God, a perfect environment, and all of the possessions he wanted, there was still a void of intimacy. Blending two individuals into oneness was the divine goal. Adam and Eve were made to become suitable counterparts who could balance and back one another in every way.

THE TWO BECOME ONE FOR A REASON.

In all of life's struggles, pain, and disappointment, you will need each other's companionship and intimacy. This intimacy develops from an attitude of servanthood in seeking to meet each other's needs and desires.

One can only have this attitude as one realizes that his or her ultimate well-being depends on God and not fully on a spouse. Only when I allow my relationship with God to be the most important relationship in my life can I find a sense of security, fulfillment, and satisfaction that does not depend on my husband's response. I can love Byron out of the love I receive from Christ and then use that love to help meet needs in his life.

God ordained marriage to be an earthly picture of the relationship between Christ and the church. Jesus Christ's love for the church, according to Ephesians 5, is sacrificial and unconditional. He laid down His life to present the church, His bride, whole and complete. Likewise, when a husband and wife love each other as they do their own bodies, nurturing and caring for each other, they live out the beautiful picture of Christ's oneness with the church.

The task of developing oneness will probably be one of the most challenging jobs you will face. Apart from a personal relationship with Jesus Christ, oneness in your marriage will never be fully realized. After all, it was God who created marriage for our well-being. Therefore, His plans, purposes, and ways can be trusted.

GOD'S PURPOSES ARE BIGGER THAN ANY WEDDING CEREMONY.

Even in the midst of God's plan, marriage is not easy. Life's disappointments and irritations combined with our own self-centeredness remind us of how much we need a Savior. It makes sense that so many marriages fail in America. Christ is not central for most couples and a consumer view of marriage is the norm; therefore, self-centeredness erodes intimacy and companionship. Without Christ, the vows promised at the altar can never be fully realized.

The key to a healthy marriage is for each of us to focus on becoming the person God created us to become. As author David Egner states, "The issue is not just what our Lord says about marriage. Solutions are found by discovering what He has said about basic issues of faith and character and then applying those perspectives to the seasons of marriage."[6]

In various ways, we are daily reminded of the first part of our marriage vows, "I take thee to be my wedded wife/husband." As we journey through the next seven sessions, our hope is for you to fully appreciate the significance of these powerful words. What an incredible privilege to be married!

SESSION 2:

ROLES *and*
RESPONSIBILITIES

WHAT'S MY PART?

OVERVIEW

The purpose of this section is to clarify, establish, and help you understand the biblical functions of a husband and a wife within marriage. These biblical principles are designed by God to provide order in the family so that there is freedom and security as we carry out the responsibilities of life.

> *"Self-centered individuality destroys oneness and companionship."*

"... TO HAVE AND TO HOLD
FROM THIS DAY FORWARD."

"A marriage may be made in heaven, but the
maintenance must be done on earth."[1]
RICHARD EXLEY

It is barely daybreak, and Ben is out the door for another long day at the office. Ben is an accountant at an emerging firm. Despite the demands of his job, Ben is energized because his business associates admire and respect him. He also knows that if he performs well he may soon be promoted to partner. So, he often works twelve to fourteen hours a day. He justifies it by saying, "Isn't it my job to provide for my family?"

As his wife, Jennifer, begins her day, she feels overwhelmed by the demands of her own job, not to mention paying the bills, maintaining order in their home, and running countless errands. Jennifer tries to be understanding, but rather than aiding and supporting Ben as a friend and helper, she feels distant and resentful. Ben and Jennifer have lost focus of what it means "to have and to hold." They have allowed screaming demands to replace sacred priorities.

In order "to have and to hold" for a lifetime, couples must grasp their unique God-given roles in marriage. Ben and Jennifer were so focused on their individual tasks that they lost sight of what is important in making a marriage function.

Taking out the trash, paying the bills, cleaning the house, mowing the grass, and cooking the meals are important tasks. Thankfully, in our marriage, we have learned what each of us does better. In our home, for example, it would be challenging for Carla to handle our finances. Her idea of a balanced checkbook is anywhere within $5 to $50, but she does enjoy preparing healthy meals. Byron's night to cook means ordering pizza—unless he makes his one and only home-cooked entrée, creamed tuna on toast. For some of our friends, though, the husband is the better cook, and the wife handles the finances. So, whose job is it? We have discovered that assigning daily responsibilities becomes secondary once we understand the foundational and functional God-designed roles in marriage.

Before the wedding day, ask: 1) What is my part? and 2) How can I contribute to making order and oneness in our family so there is freedom and security as we carry out life's responsibilities?

Creator God,

Today You have reminded me that my soul and mind need an anchor. You have created me. You have made the heavens and the earth. You have provided peace, order, and ingenious design. Be my rock. Be my fortress. Be my deliverer. You, Lord, have given me a firm place to stand. Why wouldn't I trust You? You have shown me what righteous sacrifice looks like. You have demonstrated what You value most. Lord, do I value what You value? Teach me your ways through Jesus' model. In the powerful name of Jesus, amen.

ONE

WHOSE RESPONSIBILITY IS IT TO ...?

	HOW YOU SEE IT FOR YOUR MARRIAGE			HOW YOUR PARENTS DO IT IN THEIR MARRIAGE		
	HUSBAND	WIFE	BOTH	DAD	MOM	BOTH
Manage the budget?	☐	☐	☐	☐	☐	☐
Take out the trash?	☐	☐	☐	☐	☐	☐
Communicate with extended family?	☐	☐	☐	☐	☐	☐
Wash the car?	☐	☐	☐	☐	☐	☐
Prepare the meals?	☐	☐	☐	☐	☐	☐
Make major decisions?	☐	☐	☐	☐	☐	☐
Pay the bills?	☐	☐	☐	☐	☐	☐
Change the baby's diapers?	☐	☐	☐	☐	☐	☐
Be the primary disciplinarian?	☐	☐	☐	☐	☐	☐
Wash, fold, and put away clothes?	☐	☐	☐	☐	☐	☐
Decorate for Christmas?	☐	☐	☐	☐	☐	☐
Provide income?	☐	☐	☐	☐	☐	☐
Wash and put away dishes?	☐	☐	☐	☐	☐	☐
Maintain upkeep of the car (change oil, fluids, etc.)?	☐	☐	☐	☐	☐	☐
Keep family calendar?	☐	☐	☐	☐	☐	☐
Control the remote?	☐	☐	☐	☐	☐	☐

TWO

In order to gain a broader view of roles and responsibilities, find and interview three people (if you are looking for a challenge, maybe three you do not know) and ask them the following questions.

What do you think the wife's role in marriage is?

What do you think husband's role in marriage is?

Some suggestions for possible interviewees:
- *Grocery Market Employee*
- *Friend*
- *Mall Clerk*
- *Waitress/Waiter*
- *Businessperson, Business Executive*
- *Parents*
- *Anybody who will listen and respond*

NOTE: *Attempt to leave your comfort zone in order to gain a different perspective.*

THREE

Look up the following verses to complete the chart below.

- *Genesis 1:26-27*
- *Genesis 2:18*
- *Galatians 3:28*
- *Ephesians 5:1-2, 15-33*
- *Philippians 2:1-8*
- *Colossians 3:12-21*
- *Titus 2:4-8*
- *1 Peter 3:1-7*

IDENTIFY BIBLICAL ROLES AND DUTIES		
HUSBAND	**MUTUAL**	**WIFE**

FOUR

Eat dinner together and discuss your thoughts regarding roles and responsibilities in your marriage.

Discuss how your parents fulfilled their unique roles in marriage.

In what areas do you hope to emulate your parents in your marriage?

In what areas do you plan to be different from your parents?

What did you learn about the biblical roles of a husband? Wife?

How do you imagine living this out in your marriage?

DRIVING QUESTIONS

IS THERE A DIFFERENCE BETWEEN ROLES AND RESPONSIBILITIES?

Do you plan to model the tasks/jobs (responsibilities) the same way your parents did?

What similarities exist in the way you imagine roles within your marriage being lived out and the way your parents functioned? Differences?

What issues does the Bible specifically address regarding biblical roles in marriage? What are traditional/cultural roles for each marriage partner? How are you as a couple going to determine the difference between what culture dictates and the Bible says?

In marriage, what do you see as the husband's key role? What role or function can only a husband fulfill in marriage?

In marriage, what do you see as the wife's key role? What role or function can only a wife fulfill in marriage?

"Role" does NOT denote privilege or rank for a male or female. It is more about function and order.

WHAT CAN THE MODEL OF JESUS TEACH US?

Do you desire to pattern your own life and marriage after Christ's example? Why or why not?

What words would you use to describe Jesus? Is there anything about Jesus that you would consider dishonorable? Demeaning? Disrespectful? Uncaring?

How did Christ illustrate headship? Being a helper? Submission? Praise and honor?

If Jesus perfectly modeled God's idea of both headship and submission, why does our world today often view those concepts as demeaning, disrespectful, uncaring, dishonorable, etc.?

WHAT ARE BIBLICAL ROLES?

What is involved in the husband's role of headship?

What does headship look like? Is leadership the same as headship?

Is the man (husband) required to be the spiritual leader? Is it the sole responsibility of the husband to lead spiritually or can/should the wife spiritually lead too?

Do you think men today invest more energy at work than they do in maximizing the potential of their wives and children? If so, why?

What is the wife's response to her husband's role of headship?

What is involved in the wife's role of "helper"?

What do you think it means to be a worker at home?

Do you think women today believe that building a career is more fulfilling than being a homemaker and rearing children? If so, why?

What is the husband's response to his wife's role of helper?

WHAT IS MY PART?

What do you see as the most difficult adjustment your spouse will make in living with you?

What will be the biggest change for you inn living with your (future) spouse?

Name a few married couples you know that are modeling healthy roles and responsibilities. What impresses you most in how they function?

SYNOPSIS

Every marriage settles into some type of social and organizational arrangement with both husband and wife playing specific roles. There are no role-less marriages. The noise of culture has confused God's standards and values with traditional cultural roles—even in the church. True biblical principles that provide structure, order, and function and transcend time, philosophy, and ethnicity. However, we often mistakenly attempt to adjust the Bible to support our personal mores. We should adapt to the Bible, not force the Bible to fit our lifestyles. It is obvious in Scripture that there are gender differences and diverse cultural approaches to living together as one in holy matrimony.

CORE VALUES

Keep in mind, Scripture presents some core values regarding marriage:
- Marriage deemed important (John 2:1-11)
- Monogamy and permanence in marriage (Mark 10:2-9)
- Equal responsibility (Mark 10:11-12)
- God's opposition to domination and/or deception between sexes (Matt. 5:27-30)

A WORD TO HUSBANDS

In order for unity and oneness to take place, the husband must assume the God-ordained role of headship. In 1 Corinthians 11:3 and Ephesians 5:23, the Bible says the role of headship is the husband's. The word *head* simply means "literally or figuratively the head,[2] cornerstone."[3] This functional role granted by God to man is not intended to be an abusive power position. Nor should men give into passivity that is driven by selfishness. Instead, as imitators of Christ, we are to look out for the best interest of all family members through love, nurture, and care. *Easton's Illustrated Bible Dictionary* defines husband as a "'house-band' connecting and keeping together the whole family."[4] This connection fosters maturity, while nourishing and cherishing its members.

It is not easy for the head of the home ("house-band") to lead, love, and care for his wife; he must daily die to self—as modeled by Jesus. Please know that the benefits of this sacrificial love far outweigh the costs. As I (Byron) initiate this kind of headship for Carla, she is strengthened and nourished. This motivates her to respond positively to me as she maximizes her potential and fully becomes who God intended her to be. We both find security and freedom in the oneness this creates.

A WORD TO WIVES

In Genesis 2:18, God created woman because He decided it was not good for man to be alone. In this verse, the word *helpmeet* comes from two Hebrew words. One means "to aid or help"[5] and the other means "counterpart."[6] The root derivative of *counterpart* means "a primitive root, properly, front, i.e., stand boldly out opposite."[7] Again, not a "slave" for her husband, but one who boldly stands opposite to aid or help her husband become everything God desires. Wives who offer the best aid to their husbands are those who have a deep spiritual core and find their worth, value, and security in God alone. With her mighty spiritual core, a wife can be free from the need to control and manipulate as she passionately loves and kindly serves her husband. This fosters a deeper oneness and trust

---

"The Bible presents a woman as a strong image bearer of God, able to stand against the world, powerfully influencing men and culture . . . as she lives the life God created her to live."[8]

GARY THOMAS

KIND AND COMPASSIONATE TO ONE ANOTHER

Ephesians 5 is about following Christ's example. Christ loved, gave Himself up, and sacrificed (Eph. 5:1-2). Each of these characteristics requires us to "be kind and compassionate to one another" (Eph. 4:32). To function as one, a couple must rely on God's Holy Spirit as each finds his or her role.

It is okay to work through difficult passages, such as Ephesians 5, together. This is one way God challenges our minds and transforms our lives. Keep in mind that these are radical verses from Paul to challenge men to die to self as Jesus did. Paul challenged a culture that gave men power by saying, *Use your power for the benefit of the other person.*

Before you marry one another, may God's Word challenge you first to recognize each other's value and to understand your part in making a marriage team effective. Then, you can attempt to negotiate the daily tasks of married life.

FINANCIAL RESPONSIBILITIES

HOW MUCH IS ENOUGH?

OVERVIEW

The purpose of this section is to provide a helpful overview of financial stewardship, budgeting, and money management. In order to experience true freedom, couples must gain a balanced perspective on how to deal effectively with financial responsibilities.

"We buy things we don't need with money we don't have in order to impress people we don't like."[1]

DAVE RAMSEY

"FOR BETTER FOR WORSE, FOR RICHER FOR POORER"

"God can utilize my use of His resources as a testimony to the world. My attitude as a Christian toward wealth becomes the testimony."[2]
RON BLUE

Early in our marriage, Carla was forced to take me more for the "worse and the poorer" than the "better and the richer." When my dad had to wire us money on our honeymoon, the reality of this part of the marriage vows hit us very quickly.

I often joke that it took two weeks of marriage to deplete twenty-one years of savings. As my dad reminded me, "Looks like you didn't save enough over the twenty-one years." This is a constant struggle for all of us—we spend more than we save. My dad used to tell me, "Son, it doesn't matter if you make $300 or $30,000 per month; you must discipline yourself to spend less than you make."

You may need self-discipline more in this area than in any other area covered in this study (except maybe sex). Perhaps this is why money management plays such a big part in character development. Thankfully, Scripture is full of encouragement as to how to deal with money.

"Where your treasure is, there will your heart be also."
MATTHEW 6:21, KJV

Despite the multitude of resources on money management, it seems Americans aren't getting the message. The 2016 American Household Credit Card Debt Study found that most U.S. households have an average of $134,643 in debt, including mortgages.[3] The majority of Americans live from paycheck to paycheck.[4] We have not learned the self-discipline concepts of delayed gratification and spending less than we earn.

In the first five years of marriage, a couple can either build a foundation that leads to financial freedom or bury themselves in debt and bondage that will force them to dig out over the next ten to fifteen years. After more than twenty years of working with young couples, we have observed the patterns established in those crucial first five years are determined through the behaviors of the first eighteen months of marriage.

Unless you learn and apply these financial management concepts early on, more than likely, you will experience stress in your marriage. In fact, financial difficulty (lack of compatibility in how spouses handle finances—one prefers to spend while another values saving) is one of the main reasons cited for divorce.[5]

It is important to discuss the following areas of personal finances with your partner:
- When to combine bank accounts and titles to vehicles or homes
- Planning and living on a budget
- The primary caretaker for paying bills and balancing the checkbook
- Career plans
- Long-term financial planning including life insurance and making a will
- Saving and investments

As you continue to discover and experience the best that married life has to offer, it is important to gain a balanced perspective as to how to deal effectively with financial responsibilities. Heads up, this section may be time-consuming, but it will save you time, energy, and money in the future. It will require some hard work and honesty. Keep in mind, money has a way of gut checking what we really believe to be true.

Holy God who created and owns everything,

I confess I like nice things. I like money. I like control. I like my

stuff. Oh God, please forgive me. Help me to realize You are my

Provider, and You truly know what is best. I acknowledge that

You own all. Thanks for allowing me to be Your steward,

appointed to keep order and care for Your creation. Thank You

for trusting me. It is a privilege. I am blessed. Humbly I pray,

amen.

ONE

Consider the way you manage money and material things.

What are your top two frustrations in dealing with money?
1.

2.

List your strengths and weaknesses regarding your financial life:

STRENGTHS   WEAKNESSES

Look at your life and family heritage in financial matters:

The right attitudes and actions I learned growing up:

The wrong attitudes and actions I learned growing up:

TWO

Please work together as a couple. This may take some time.

Step 1: Where are you?

- List the debt each of you is bringing into the marriage. Look at Assignment #3.
- Establish a working budget for your first year of marriage. Complete the Personal Budget worksheet in the appendix (p.106).

Step 2: Where do you want to be?

- Compare your budget with the Percentage Guide in the appendix (p.108).
- Discuss the differences between your percentages and what is recommended.

Step 3: How do we get there?

- Determine a way to increase your cash flow margin.
- On a separate piece of paper, list your financial goals. Remember: the higher the cash flow margin, the faster you will attain financial freedom.

Step 4: How do we stay there?

- Control your monthly cash flow by frequently reviewing your budget. Find a simple method. Delegate responsibility for each area of the budget.
- After six months of marriage, consider working through the first three steps again.

NOTE: *Keep in mind, the first five years of your marriage financially are dependent on how you manage money in your first eighteen months of marriage.*

THREE

DEBT: THE DANGER TRAP

Look up the following Scriptures that speak about debt. Journal your thoughts.

- *Psalm 37:21*

- *Proverbs 22:7*

- *Luke 14:28*

- *Romans 13:8*

- *James 4:13-17*

FOUR

TWO PRIMARY DANGERS OF DEBT

1. Debt always presumes upon the future. List your current debt. Write down how much you owe and what you owe it for.

I OWE	THIS MUCH
Car payment	$300

How are we going to pay this off?

2. Debt may deny God an opportunity to work.

How do you think God as Father wants to take care of His children?

Is God meeting your needs financially? Why or why not?

Are you giving Him the opportunity to do so?

What is one thing you can do to improve your financial situation?

What are some financial expectations you have for your marriage?

WHAT ARE YOUR CONCERNS ABOUT FINANCES?

What are some of your common frustrations concerning money matters?

Does money stress you out? Does money control you? What are your biggest concerns with the way your (future) spouse handles finances?

*What challenges do you think you will face as a couple going from **my** money to **our** money?*

Do you have concerns about your debt? Your partner's debt?

Why do you think money is one of the major causes for divorce in our country?

Should both husband and wife work outside of the home? What if children were to enter the family?

LET'S TALK BUDGETING.

Who handled the money in your family growing up? Mom? Dad? Both? Neither? Who will be primarily responsible for your finances in your new family?

Are you a saver or a spender? What do you expect from your (future) spouse?

Is shopping a privilege, right, or chore?

What happens if your money runs out before your expenses do?

As a couple, did you come up with ways to save money? Do you have a financial plan (or goals) for your marriage?

HAVE YOU DISCUSSED DEBT?

When (if ever) do you borrow?

Debt presumes on the future and may deny God an opportunity to work. How do you plan to move forward concerning debt?

How do you get out of debt?

WHAT DOES THE BIBLE SAY ABOUT MONEY?

Read each passage and sum it up with one phrase:

Ecclesiastes 5:10

Matthew 23:23

1 Timothy 6:6-11

Christ never said money or material things were problems. But, He said the love of money can be the root of all kinds of problems.

Read Luke 12:15-21. What did Jesus identify as more important than material possessions?

It surprises many Christians to learn that approximately two-thirds of the parables that Christ used in His teaching deal specifically with finances, the things we own, and how we utilize the resources God has given us.[6]

Christ constantly warned us to guard our hearts against greed, covetousness, ego, and pride because these are some of the tools that Satan uses to control and manipulate this world.

DO YOU TRUST GOD TO BE YOUR PROVIDER?

In what specific ways do you trust our faithful God to provide for you?

What do you know or what have you learned regarding stewardship?

What are your financial goals for the present? In one to three years? Twenty years? Forty years?

SYNOPSIS

WE NEED HELP

The first step to financial freedom is to acknowledge that your loving, sovereign God owns it all. Money has a unique way of asking, "What do you believe about God?" and then showing your answer by the way you live.

Jesus seemed to believe that the way a person manages financial resources is an outward indicator of important character traits. In Matthew 6:21, Jesus said "For where your treasure is, there your heart will be also." Every person has the privilege of managing the resources God has entrusted to him or her.

At several points in our marriage, we have been challenged by circumstances that caused us to see whether we really believed God owns all and controls all. When our two-year-old son battled cancer, God used His people, the church, to meet every need we faced. From meals to massive medical bills, our church family acknowledged that God owns and controls everything. God's people responded in obedience to His prompting and helped provide for our financial needs.

After two years of chemotherapy, radiation, surgery, more than one hundred hospital stays, and countless doctor's appointments, we concluded our experience without owing one penny. It was truly miraculous considering our meager youth ministry salary. Realistically, we could not have paid a fraction of the cost out of our own resources, yet God provided and His people obeyed. We learned a valuable lesson about God's provision—up close and personal. We also learned the equally important visual lesson in obedience.

REAL PERSPECTIVE

Our heavenly Father provides guiding principles for us so that we might be trusted to care for all His creation. With the transfer of wealth comes responsibility. Hopefully this motivates you to understand stewardship, budgeting, money management, and how to deal effectively with financial matters.

It has been said that how one spends his or her time and money reveals true character. God can use our finances to mold us into His image, complete with self-control, patience, faithfulness, and honesty.

FINANCIAL FREEDOM

Remember, God owns it all! Money is never an end in and of itself but merely a resource used to accomplish other goals and commitments. There is always a trade-off between time and effort, money and rewards. If we spend less than we earn and do so for a long time, we will be financially successful. Delayed gratification is the key.

Money is one of the resources God uses to accomplish the real goals and objectives of life. As you struggle with your budget, overspending, and major spending decisions, rest assured that all of these struggles are spiritual development tools. Money can form you into the image of God, or it can deform you with worry, stress, and out-of-control living. The challenge is not to plan God out of your finances. He wants to complete a good work in you. Trust Him. He knows what He is doing. We must do our part—obey!

My dad may not have been surprised by my honeymoon plea from Mexico. But, through it all, learning how to manage our finances has helped Carla and me become more responsible individuals, fully committed to one another for better for worse, for richer for poorer.

EMOTIONAL INTIMACY

HOW DO WE MAINTAIN A CONNECTION?

OVERVIEW

The purpose of this section is to challenge your thinking regarding emotional needs, intimacy, and oneness in marriage. We want to help you establish a strong commitment in marriage that lovingly fulfills these emotional needs. Love is based on a commitment of the will, not a passing feeling.

> *"Deep emotional intimacy is when we feel wholly accepted, respected, and admired in the eyes of our mate even when they know our innermost struggles and failures."*[1]
>
> **JILL SAVAGE**

"IN SICKNESS AND IN HEALTH, TO LOVE, HONOR, AND CHERISH, TILL DEATH DO US PART."

"A good marriage isn't something you find;
it's something you make."[2]
GARY THOMAS

When Byron and I (Carla) were engaged, we would go to dinner and see married couples sitting in silence. Sometimes the husband would be reading the newspaper. We would stand in judgment, wondering how they could let their marriage become so b-o-r-i-n-g. We knew *that* would never happen to *us*. We believed that our relationship would always be fueled by the intense romantic feelings we felt during our engagement, and conversation would always flow easily. Now, after years of marriage, we are not so quick to judge. As a matter of fact, we have found ourselves at restaurants struggling to find something to talk about besides our children. The temptation to pull out the newspaper is real. Or better yet, the temptation to both become captivated by the screens of our electronic devices.

Needless to say, we have realized in our own marriage that intimacy and romance do not just happen. Intimacy requires a commitment to love each other in spite of the disappointments and difficulties we face. The marriage vows "in sickness and health, to love, honor, and cherish, till death do us part" promise a lifelong commitment.

How will you keep your marriage exciting and deepen your love for your mate in years to come? This is one of the important questions for you to address as you begin a new marriage.

In many relationships, once the honeymoon is over, the marriage slowly becomes lukewarm. Each spouse gradually begins to take the other for granted. Days turn into months, and months turn into years. For many couples, what began as a close and intimate relationship disintegrates. Often two people are simply living under the same roof—sharing a bed, bathroom, and closet—physically in the same home, yet miles apart emotionally.

The purpose of this section is to challenge your thinking regarding emotional needs, intimacy, and oneness in marriage. We want to help you establish a strong commitment in marriage that lovingly fulfills these needs. Love is based on a commitment of the will, not a passing feeling.

Dear patient and holy Father,

Since life is filled with busyness and responsibilities, it's easy to forget that marriage is a welcomed sigh of relief that brings security. Help us to enjoy one another's company as we have fun together and meet each other's needs. Please help us to keep the friendship and fun alive in our marriage. Show us when we should step up and boldly enter the other's world. Please guide our hearts to connect on deeper levels. In Jesus' name we pray, amen.

"He is altogether lovely. This is my beloved, and this is my friend ..."
SONG OF SOLOMON 5:16, NKJV

ONE

Complete the following sentences. (This will be fun to save and look back on ten years from now.)

Our favorite song is:

Our favorite place to eat together is:

One of our greatest memories together is:

The characteristic that attracted me the most to my future mate was:

TWO

> Dating is meant to conceal,
> marriage is meant to reveal.

Oftentimes people enter marriage plagued by some degree of personal self-doubt and insecurity. Usually they carefully mask it behind performance and denial.

Read the following verses and consider this question: how will you respond when your mate's weaknesses and flaws are revealed?

- *Romans 15:1-7*

- *1 Corinthians 13:4-8*

- *Philippians 2:3-4*

- *Colossians 3:12-15*

THREE

Dr. Gary Chapman's best seller, The Five Love Languages, *can help you express your heartfelt commitment to one another. Take his free love language assessment online at 5lovelanguages.com. Then, take some time to learn more about the five love languages. Apply what you learn below:*

NOTE: *The way you receive love is usually the way you give love too.*

What is the primary way you give love? Receive love?

How does your (future) spouse give love? Receive love?

Reading about these five patterns, I discovered ...

Do something creative and out of the ordinary to communicate your love for your (future) spouse this week. For example, send her a rose with a note telling her how committed you are to her. Blindfold him and take him to a fun place you have never been before. Note: Remember to speak your partner's love language—not your own.

NOTE: *For further study of the five love languages, read* The Five Love Languages *by Dr. Gary Chapman.*

FOUR

Complete the Top Ten Commonly Identified Intimacy Needs worksheet (See the appendix, p.109.)

Summarize your top three intimacy needs in a few sentences.
Need:

Need:

Need:

Go for coffee and discuss these needs. Attempt to describe what each of your needs looks like and how your (future) spouse can best help meet those needs. Take time to listen as your (future) spouse describes his or her top three intimacy needs and how you can best serve him or her.

DRIVING QUESTIONS

CAN YOU LIVE WITH THEM?
CAN THEY LIVE WITH YOU?

Name two or three of your "good" habits. Name two or three of your "annoying" habits. How do you feel about your partner's habits?

Do you respect and accept each other's habits and baggage? If not, why is it so difficult for you? Is there a particular issue that trips you up?

How much "me time" do you need? Do you think your partner will respect and allow your "me time"?

What creates the most stress in your life? What causes the greatest frustration in your life?

How have you seen your (future) spouse handle stress, frustration, and anger? Is this a response you can live with? Why or why not?

If you are blessed with children, would you want them to follow this model?

Name some of the ways you plan to deepen your relationship with your spouse in the years to come.

CAN YOU BE VULNERABLE?

What did you learn about meeting each other's needs from Prep Work Assignment #4?

What is the easiest emotion for you to experience?
What is the most difficult?

What makes it easier for you to be open and vulnerable?
What makes it difficult?

Can your partner be vulnerable? Why or why not?

If vulnerability doesn't happen during dating or courtship or engagement, then how do you think it will be different in marriage?

With what part of giving of yourself do you struggle the most?

How can a wife positively show honor to her husband?

How can a husband demonstrate to his wife that he cherishes her?

ARE YOU WILLING TO LOVE EACH OTHER SACRIFICIALLY AND UNCONDITIONALLY?

In what ways has your partner demonstrated unconditional love?

When someone close to you is sick, how do you currently respond? When you are sick, how do you want your spouse to respond?

What are some things (tangible or intangible) you have forfeited or given up for the sake of your (future) spouse?

Jesus is the ultimate model of unconditional and sacrificial love. List five descriptive words that characterize Jesus' life and might offer guidance to your relationship.

HOW DO YOU PLAN TO KEEP THE ROMANCE GOING AFTER MARRIAGE?

Do you feel more emotionally connected now than you did early in your relationship? If yes, how? If no, what can you do to nurture that emotional intimacy?

How would you define love? How does this definition compare with what we thought love was in the past?

SYNOPSIS

"Things which matter most must never be at the mercy of things which matter least."[3]

JOHANN WOLFGANG VON GOETHE

As a married couple, the norm is to share a bedroom, bank account, and kids yet seldom connect on a deeper level. The undercurrent of daily life pulls you into self-centeredness. The sin of selfishness can lead to isolation and destroy your marriage. However, by yielding our lives to Christ, who gave His life to rescue us from our selfish desires, we are able to build a strong and intimate marriage. Trust and dependence on God's love enable you to stay connected and committed not only when it's easy but for a lifetime. Again, we remind you that it is so worth it—marriage is remarkable!

GOD'S PLAN FOR INTIMACY

In Genesis 2:18-25, God saw that it was not good for mankind to be alone. Even though Adam had a perfect environment, perfect position, and a perfect relationship with God, he was isolated.

The older I (Byron) get, the more I realize being fully vulnerable and "naked" emotionally and spiritually, as well as physically, brings about true intimacy—into-me-see (simple definition of intimacy).[4] Carla sees everything about my life and still accepts me. The beauty of the marriage covenant is that each individual promises never to leave nor forsake the other.

HOW DO ROMANCE AND INTIMACY ERODE?

Laziness can erode intimacy and romance. It is easy to take the faithfulness of your mate for granted. It is also easy to become lazy in meeting each other's needs, settling instead for the mundane and mediocre.

Early in marriage, tenderness, romance, and thoughtfulness are instinctive and come naturally. Later, though, they require discipline and commitment. For many couples, rather than spending the effort to meet each other's needs, the demands of careers, kids, and individual needs become the focus of the marriage.

HELPFUL SUGGESTIONS

A newly married couple can avoid the trap of laziness and truly seek to meet each other's needs by purposefully giving priority to time with one another each week. Other people and events will try to crowd out your time together. In making time for each other, you will say *no* to many very good things. But, you will be saying *yes* to maintaining an intimate, healthy marriage.

Work hard to become a student of your spouse. I am motivated to get a Ph.D. in "Carla-ology." Remember: women and men are very different in both their desires for intimacy and their ideas of romance.

It is important to openly and honestly communicate each of your desires. Both of you should strive to listen to each other, to truly understand each other's love language, and then begin to find creative ways of communicating love to one another. Never forget the incredible value of your spouse.

May the commitment you make at the altar "in sickness and in health, to love, honor, and cherish, till death do us part" become a reality as your love deepens over the years. Most of all, may you never bury your head in the newspaper or electronic device on a dinner date!

SPIRITUAL INTIMACY

CAN TWO REALLY BECOME ONE SPIRITUALLY?

OVERVIEW

The purpose of this section is to encourage and challenge individuals to pursue godly character and discipline. We also hope to help couples relate on a spiritual basis as oneness occurs. As your relationship matures, spiritual oneness will be the foundation to emotional connection and physical passion.

"The sanctity of marriage necessitates personal commitment—necessity of commitment is weakened by our sinful nature; and our sinful nature can be counteracted by Jesus Christ."[1]

DR. CHARLES SWINDOLL

"ACCORDING TO GOD'S HOLY ORDINANCES"

"When first things are put first, second things
are not suppressed but increased."[2]

C.S. LEWIS

Most of us are looking for a simple formula we can use to follow God's holy ordinances. Sadly, many Christians are just religious enough to be miserable, making God's ordinances legalities that exasperate us. As religious people, we live with a certain amount of traditional, ceremonial, and dogmatic behavior. We do it automatically. When we were children, we were taught to behave and even think in a prescribed way. If we're simply going through the motions, do we really experience spiritual growth when we go to church, do good deeds, pray, make good moral decisions, meditate, and so forth? To answer that question, it is important to attempt to define *spiritual growth*.

Traditional ways can be important to the process, but true spiritual growth occurs when the Spirit of God is made known in our lives and our egos shrink. In some ways, spiritual growth is a misnomer. The Spirit does not grow or shrink; He remains the way He is, never changing. Further, spiritual growth happens only in direct relationship to a diminishing of our ego. The ego refers to my self-centered qualities that determine decisions based solely on what is best for me. My reasoning is based upon my needs—I, I, I, me, me, me. In contrast, for true spiritual growth to occur, we must come to realize that God is the center of the universe—not me, my marriage, or my wedding. We should probably rename this section *ego diminishing*. Entering into a marriage covenant is a great way to experience ego shrinkage.

If someone had pulled us aside during our engagement or early days of marriage and told us that living out this part of the marriage vow would be one of the greatest challenges to oneness in our marriage, we would have denied it. But, when the honeymoon was over, we began to realize the complexity of growing together in Christ. Reluctantly we have recognized that our struggle is due to individual selfishness, ego, and pride. Spiritual growth takes place daily—adding to the difficulty. In other areas, such as money, in-laws, and even communication, you can usually take a break for a couple of days. But spiritual growth is so dynamic, it demands constant attention and learning about one another.

As this session challenges you to pursue godly character and discipline, our hope is that spiritual oneness will occur. Only when you begin to understand yourself and, more importantly, God will you begin to understand and experience how two can really become one spiritually.

"Most High, Most Glorious God,

Enlighten the darkness of my heart,

Grant me a right and true faith,

A certain hope, and

A perfect charity, feeling, and understanding,

Of You,

So that I may be able to accomplish

Your holy and just commands.

Amen."

—St. Francis of Assisi [3]

ONE

These diagnostic questions may help you assess your degree of spiritual oneness as a couple.

Is your (future) spouse supportive and encouraging of your personal spiritual growth?

Do you regularly practice the spiritual disciplines of confession and forgiveness (with God and with your church community)?

Do you often talk about important issues concerning values and beliefs?

Do you regularly pray together?

It's possible for a couple to be made of two spiritual giants
who lack spiritual intimacy with one another.

TWO

Part I: List five values you hold as most important. What will you not compromise?

1.

2.

3.

4.

5.

Compare lists with your partner. Ask your partner to further explain each item listed. Talk through the reason for his or her choices. Discuss your differences.

Does his or her expenditure of time match his or her top five values?

How can you help your (future) spouse live according to his or her values?

Part II: Share in detail with your (future) mate how and when Christ became the center of your life. How has Christ impacted your life? Specifically how is God working in your life right now?[4]

Part III: Pray together.

THREE

If this is a hectic week, call each other and discuss the following questions. If time allows, go on a bike ride or walk and discuss the following questions.

Read Matthew 6:33 and ask each other the following questions.

What is His kingdom? What is not His kingdom?

How do you seek His kingdom? Name potential roadblocks you might face in the first year of your marriage.

What are "these things" mentioned in the Matthew 6 passage?

Why does verse 33 begin with the word "but"?

How can this serve as an anchor throughout marriage as each of you grows and changes?

FOUR

Read through the following suggestions and discuss how you can currently implement some of them in your relationship. This week, select one or two practical ways you can experience spiritual oneness.

PRACTICAL SUGGESTIONS FOR SPIRITUAL GROWTH AS A COUPLE

- *Pray together daily.*
- *Study the Bible and worship together.*
- *Develop a meaningful Sabbath rest experience—practice it regularly.*
- *Have a Sabbath meal; center your conversation around Jesus Christ.*
- *Connect with a church.*
- *Disciple/mentor a younger couple.*
- *Participate in a mission/service project.*
- *Plan a silent retreat (at least one hour); then, discuss your thoughts after the retreat.*
- *Practice the discipline of fasting together for a day; then, try it for a week.*
- *On a road trip, memorize a lengthy passage of Scripture.*
- *Experience confession and forgiveness from both sides—often!*
- *Read a challenging book and discuss each chapter.*
- *Go on a prayer walk.*
- *Keep a journal for a month and share your thoughts and writing.*
- *Spend a quiet evening together listening to worship music.*
- *Pull away for an extended time of personal evaluation once or twice a year; take a spiritual inventory.*
- *Spend a Sabbath weekend away assessing your Christian life and evaluating your growth as a couple. Ask each other questions. Allow God to search you and know your thoughts, actions, and attitudes. Commit to renewed growth in areas of weakness that God reveals.*

NOTE: *Don't feel pressure to practice the entire list immediately. This list is intended to be a helpful guide for you throughout your marriage.*

DRIVING QUESTIONS

WHAT IS SPIRITUAL GROWTH?

How does God measure spiritual growth? Why is it important in marriage?

What do you think the phrase "discipline brings freedom" means?

As a (soon-to-be) married person, what would you receive spiritually from marriage that you would not as a single person?

In your opinion, how does a person measure whether he or she is growing spiritually?

WHY ARE SPIRITUAL DISCIPLINES IMPORTANT IN A MARRIAGE?

How would you define spiritual formation? Why it is important in a marriage?

Is it easy or difficult to pray with one another? Why?

As a couple, how much does the Bible inform the principles that guide your lives?

DO YOU RELATE TO GOD IN THE SAME WAY?

Please see the handout "How We Relate to God" in the appendix (p.110). Identify one or two pathways which most resonate with you. Discuss the similarities and differences between your preferences and those of your (future) spouse.

Do each of you relate to God in the same way?

What do you desire from your mate regarding spiritual connection?

What could you do to help yourself worship more deeply on a regular basis?

WHY IS SPIRITUAL ONENESS THE FOUNDATION OF A HEALTHY MARRIAGE AND HOME?

What does it mean to be a spiritual leader? Is spiritual leadership solely the responsibility of the husband? How does one become a spiritual leader?

Why do most young couples wait until after their children come along to connect with a local church? ?

How involved in a local church do you plan to be? Are you on the same page with your (future) spouse regarding church participation? Why or why not? What would it take to be on the same page?

Why is physical passion tied so closely to spiritual oneness?

A NOTE FOR ENGAGED COUPLES

The more a couple prays together, the closer they become. During your engagement, be cautious and intentional to guard your physical purity. Couples wonder why it is so difficult during engagement to control physical passions. The physical body does not know the difference between being married or unmarried, but the spirit, mind, and emotion certainly know the distinction.

It is good to grow in spiritual oneness. But be aware that the more the spirit and soul connect in oneness, the more quickly the body's natural reactions will follow.

SYNOPSIS

In my life, I (Byron) can point to three areas that have assisted me in diminishing my ego and, thus, growing spiritually. Developing personal discipline, attempting to understand true *agape* love, and struggling through hardship have deepened my faith in Jesus Christ as I strived to live according to God's holy ordinances. In the process, Carla and I have sharpened one another as "iron sharpens iron" (Prov. 27:17). We have learned to appreciate each other's qualities and have found a healthy balance in pursuing God together. We have found again and again in our marriage that our relationships with God are foundational to our journey toward oneness.

PERSONAL DISCIPLINE AS AN AVENUE TO ONENESS

A year and a half after our wedding, my faith journey felt like I was sprinting on a treadmill. Spiritually, I was working harder and moving faster, doing things religiously, yet not making any ground in knowing, understanding, and living out biblical principles. I was so busy doing things for God and attempting to impress God that I completely missed God in the process. *Ordering Your Private World* by Gordon MacDonald changed my approach to life. For the first time in my life as a Christian, I realized that discipline brings freedom. As I began to practice inner spiritual disciplines, God's Spirit changed my life.

Over the years I have observed that busyness is one of the biggest distractions to growing in Christ. Busy, busy, busy. I am *so busy*! *Merriam-Webster's* dictionary defines *busy* as being "engaged in action; full of activity; foolishly or intrusively active; or full of distracting detail."[5] If we are not careful, busyness can easily become cluttered activity with minute detail that distracts us from the focal point. Did you catch that? Cluttered activity that distracts attention from the focal point.

In order to make Christ a major priority in your life, and thus your marriage, you must eliminate the cluttered activity that distracts you from the focal point—Jesus Christ is our focus. The disciplines of prayer, Bible study, fasting, Sabbath rest, solitude, and simplicity can take you off the treadmill and move you forward toward gainful activity.

UNDERSTANDING TRUE LOVE AS AN AVENUE TO ONENESS

As I strive to become less egocentric and more Christ-focused, I realize how much my marriage relationship facilitates my spiritual growth. My relationship with Carla is a constant opportunity for me to live out the truths I believe about God. I can't drum up enough feeling or motivation to love Carla long-term without being empowered by the Holy Spirit. God's Spirit enables me to comprehend patience, kindness, goodness, faithfulness, gentleness, and self-control. If these qualities, listed in Galatians 5:22-23, are let loose in our lives, then we experience oneness in marriage.

ONENESS BENEFITS

As you consider growing in the knowledge of Christ, there are no easy conditional formulas of "do this and then this will happen." Spiritual growth will be one of the toughest issues you face in your marriage because it requires dying to self. But the perks of spiritual oneness are well worth the sacrifice. As part of you diminishes, it is replaced with character qualities from an Almighty God.

As the two of you take on Christlike qualities, you will experience life change. Spiritual oneness:

- Deepens your conversation and thought level with one another.

- Deepens your intimacy with one another.

- Increases your commitment and compatibility with one another.

- Increases your capacity to express love for one another.

Personally living according to God's holy ordinances is the greatest thing you can do for your marriage.

SESSION 6:

PHYSICAL INTIMACY

HOW DO WE ACHIEVE SEXUAL INTIMACY?

OVERVIEW

The purpose of this section is to educate couples regarding various aspects, myths, and expectations of sexual intimacy. "And they shall become one flesh" (Gen. 2:24, NASB).

"Getting married for sex is like buying a 747 for the free peanuts."[1]
JEFF FOXWORTHY

"THE TWO SHALL BECOME ONE FLESH."

"Sex is a total body experience—not a contact sport."
ANONYMOUS

Statistics indicate the average couple experiences sex two to three times per week.[2] When most men enter marriage, their sexual expectations are much higher than the average. Honestly, my (Byron) picture of our honeymoon and first years of marriage included having sex all or most of every day. But three children and several years into marriage, I would have modified the statistical evidence to read "one to two hours per week, if they are fortunate—and don't have small children."

One young man in our class took it on as a personal challenge to increase the national statistical average of time spent in sexual activity. The truth is that sex is only a fraction of the whole sum of marriage. Although a small part, sexual intimacy is a powerful, exciting, and significant component that brings intimacy with your spouse to new levels.

There are 168 hours in a week and the average couple spends only a small portion of that time in sexual activity. It did not take me long as a new husband to realize that those one to two hours of sexual activity a week were completely dependent on the other 166. Rest, nutrition, stress, work schedules, money concerns, communication, spiritual attitudes, dirty clothes, dishwashing, and giving one another undivided attention, among other things, all factor into the equation. Certainly, the non-sexual activities of the day are vital for a couple to experience meaningful, sexual intimacy.

Obviously, God created male and female distinctly different. Both men and women have sexual desires, but making love meets these needs in a different way for each partner. Comedian Jerry Seinfeld accurately states, "The basic conflict between men and women, sexually, is that men are like firemen. To men, sex is an emergency, and no matter what we're doing we can be ready in two minutes.

Women, on the other hand, are like fire. They're very exciting, but the conditions have to be exactly right."[3]

CONFORMING TO THE PATTERNS OF THIS WORLD

Although sex is a hot topic in our society, I am convinced most of us have been misinformed and/or undereducated regarding human sexuality. Most men and women lack a good factual understanding of the issues pertaining to a healthy sexual relationship with their spouses. In addition, many myths continue to be passed on as truth. Undereducation and misinformation serve as barriers, or at least hindrances, to our fully experiencing what God created to be a sanctified sexual relationship.

Thus, it is critical to grasp that God created sexual intimacy to be a beautiful and sacred part of the husband and wife relationship. Our physical bodies and the act of physical love are the pure and divine creations of a perfect and loving God. The biblical premise of God's perfect creation forms the foundation of any discussion about our sensual natures. Therefore, any time human sexuality is given a dirty or nasty connotation, we must understand it as a lie and a distortion of God's creation.

In contradiction God's truth, our cultural misinformation encourages premarital, extramarital, or perverted sexual relationships. The Bible gives specific instruction to avoid such relationships. This instruction is designed to protect and provide for us in order that we might experience true intimacy with others. God created us to need real, life-giving, intimate relationships—not selfish, physical passion that deceives and robs us of life.

Before you physically consummate the marriage, it is vital for you to use your brain to think through truths, myths, and expectations. As this session prepares the two of you to become one flesh, be sure—for now—only your mind and your soul are brought to the discussion.

Oh God,

Please do not allow temptation to overtake us. We know that it is common for humankind to struggle sexually; yet, we know that You, oh God, are faithful. You will not allow us to be tempted beyond what we can withstand; but with the temptation, You will provide the way of escape so that we will be able to endure it. Teach us Your truth about sexuality. Guide our thoughts, guard our hearts, and help our minds and spirits be in step with You so that our bodies do not deceive us. Thank You for such a creative gift. You have blessed husband and wife. More than ever, we need Your power, so we pray this in the power of Jesus. Amen.

PREP WORK

ONE

This assignment was intentionally left blank in order to remind you to avoid all sexual activities or any practical application until after your wedding day!

TWO

Read, study, and pray the following Scriptures:

- *Genesis 1:27-28*
- *Genesis 2:24-25*
- *Proverbs 5:15-19*
- *Song of Solomon 4:9-12*
- *Song of Solomon 7:6-10*
- *Song of Solomon 8:6-7*
- *Matthew 19:5-6*
- *1 Corinthians 7:2-5*
- *1 Thessalonians 4:3-8*
- *Hebrews 13:4*

Why are many people confused about sex and its role?

What was the intended role of sex as given by God?

Why is it critical that sex be experienced only between marital partners?

Write out one question regarding sexuality and the opposite sex that you'd really like to ask your (future) spouse. Pray and think about how best to ask it.

THREE

Discuss the following with your (future) spouse:

- *Any hurtful past sexual experiences*
- *Appropriate degree of sexual intimacy during your engagement*
- *Premarital intercourse*
- *Birth Control*
- *Demonstrations of affection*
- *Expectations of a good sex life within marriage*

From your point of view, a perfect sexually intimate time on your honeymoon night would include:

How often do you want to enjoy an intimate evening with each other?

Review and compare your answers with those of your partner.

FOUR

Read through the Sexual Intimacy Q&A in the appendix on page 112. Then, discuss any questions or concerns you may have had with your (future) spouse.

List some of your observations below.

What was it like talking about this topic together?

After your discussion, pray seriously for God to empower you with His Spirit to demonstrate self-control and love.

DRIVING QUESTIONS

IS OUR CULTURE SENDING CONFUSING MESSAGES ABOUT SEX?

Why do you think our society is consumed with sex?

Is it possible that we have been both miseducated and undereducated about human sexuality? How?

Why do many Christians have trouble giving themselves permission to celebrate and have a great time in the sensuous pleasures of married love?

How can our sex lives teach us valuable lessons in our spiritual lives?

What is one sexual myth you have believed in the past?

WHAT ARE SOME HINDRANCES YOU SEE FACING NEWLYWEDS?

Why do you think God made men and women so differently in how long it takes them to become sexually stimulated?

Do you wish you had a better understanding of healthy sexual relationships? Where did you learn the most about sex?

If one person in a marital relationship is more willing to learn about sex than the other, what does this tell you?

What unhealthy messages did you receive about sex when you were younger?

What questions do you have?

WHAT SHOULD WE EXPECT ON OUR WEDDING NIGHT?

What are you most looking forward to on your wedding night?

Read "The Wedding Night" found in Song of Solomon 4:1–5:1. As you read these poetic words, what insight did you gain?

Are there any considerations we need to take into account to enhance our first sexual experience together?

What can we do to keep from being so exhausted on the week of our wedding?

If you are married for fifty years, you will have 18,250 nights together. How does this realization take the pressure off of "the first night"? What are some ways you can relax, laugh, and enjoy being married, naked, and unashamed?

If you have had sex before, how do you deal with the fact that this is not your first time? How can you make your wedding night special as you consummate your marriage?

DO YOU HAVE A PLAN TO REMAIN PHYSICALLY PURE?

If you are virgins, should you wait until you are married for your sexual relationship? If you have been sexually active as a couple, is it important that you stop sexual activity until after your wedding? Do you know what the Lord says about this in His Word?

Read 1 Thessalonians 4:3-8. Why do you think that the writer speaks about sanctification and sex in the same passage? What does it look like to abstain from sexual immorality?

How do you plan to control your own body now?
Throughout your marriage?

What are your beliefs about pornography? Has pornography ever been a part of your life? If so, how recently? Take time to have an honest conversation with one another. How can your marriage partner help you in this area?

HOW WILL SEX INFLUENCE OUR FUTURE?

Do we really understand what a healthy sexual relationship looks like? How can this affect our future?

Is it important for what happens in the bedroom to stay in the bedroom?

How many children would we like to have someday? How long should we wait before we try to get pregnant or adopt?

Have we discussed birth control with one another and our physicians? What are our options?

How would a baby change our lives?

SYNOPSIS

God designed the wonderful blessing of physical intimacy to be a gift freely given to one's spouse. The key is that you give freely, no strings attached, to meet your spouse's needs. It is not something you do ("Did you do it?") or get ("Did you get some?") but something you share and give. This kind of giving is motivated by unconditional love. In 1 Corinthians 7:3-5, Paul speaks frankly about the issue of lovemaking when he indicates neither spouse has ownership over his or her own body in the marriage relationship. Rather, they are each to give of themselves to the other partner as there is need.

> "The husband should fulfill his marital duty to his wife, and likewise the wife to her husband. The wife's body does not belong to her alone but also to her husband. In the same way, the husband's body does not belong to him alone but also to his wife. Do not deprive each other except perhaps by mutual consent and for a time, so that you may devote yourselves to prayer. Then come together again so that Satan will not tempt you because of your lack of self-control."
>
> **1 CORINTHIANS 7:3-5**

If, however, one or both spouses begin to withhold the enjoyment of sexual intimacy from the other, tension and eventually some degree of bitterness could develop in the relationship. To avoid miscommunication, it is imperative for each spouse to communicate openly and honestly about physical desires and needs.

Also, within marriage, sexual relations are to be regular. As verse five says, "come together again so that Satan will not tempt you because of your lack of self-control." Although there is no ideal number of times per week, month, or year for a couple to engage in sexual intimacy, a guiding principle is to sexually "come together" regularly in order to meet one another's needs and so you are not tempted to look elsewhere for sexual fulfillment.

IT LASTS A LIFETIME.

Lastly, learn to be patient with one another. You have a lifetime to enjoy each other sexually. Our culture would like to convince you that sexually everything takes place naturally, but this is a half-truth. More realistically, sexual intimacy is a trial and error process that develops over the course of your marriage. In other words, do not expect to have great, ultimate sex on your honeymoon night. Rather, expect to enjoy the process of being naked and not ashamed (Gen. 2:25). Then over the next fifty years of marriage, you can work toward great sex.

Remember, sex is not a seven-minute experience; it is an all-day affair. Thus, perfecting life during those 166 hours a week will help you experience the ultimate in sexual intimacy. The awesome part is God wired us that way.

We do recognize that many people bring baggage and sexual hurts into a marriage. Finding help and healing is important for your marriage. Don't hesitate to reach out to a local pastor or Christian counselor should you want to work through past hurts with someone.

COMMUNICATION *and* CONFLICT MANAGEMENT

CAN WE LEARN TO TALK AND FIGHT EFFECTIVELY FOR OUR MARRIAGE?

OVERVIEW

The purpose of this section is to understand the communication skills involved in managing conflict in your relationship. Communication is the lifeblood of every marriage. Since conflict is inevitable, a married couple needs ways to safely and respectfully work through issues. These principles are key to developing a healthy marriage.

> *"It takes two to speak the truth—one to speak, and another to hear."*[1]
>
> **HENRY DAVID THOREAU**

KEYS TO LIVING OUT THE VOWS

"Conflict is like water: too much causes damage to people and property; too little creates a dry, barren landscape devoid of life and color."[2]
CONSTANTINO AND MERCHANT

Is it any wonder that communication is such a tough issue? We all differ in personality and temperament, values and philosophies, background and history. Our attempts to communicate are filtered through these discrepancies. Don't assume that love alone, without skills and understanding, will produce a successful marriage.

Byron and I (Carla) are very aware of how challenging it can be to communicate, especially when our differences enter into the conversation. Just recently we had one of those late night conversations where we completely misfired. Actually, it began early in the evening but ended very late in the evening or early in the morning. We each had our own opinions, and our opinions differed. We were both determined to get our points across. As the discussion progressed and intensified, I slipped into my usual pattern of withdrawing into my "turtle shell." Some people say silence is golden, but in this case, silence was destructive. Byron tends to escalate; so the quieter I got, the more frustrated Byron became.

After a couple of hours of difficult conversation, I realized I needed to consider Byron's point of view. I needed to let go of my pride, truly listen, and seek to understand his heart. Silently avoiding the issue was counterproductive. As we faced the issue, Byron softened his tone; I clearly communicated my thoughts. This allowed Byron to better understand my side of the issue. We had to deny our natural tendencies and focus our efforts on managing the issue. Eventually we worked through our disagreement. Conflict is never fun, but God uses it to whittle away our rough edges, conform us more to His image, and deeply bond us with one another.

BEST PREDICTOR OF FUTURE MARRIAGES

Communicating and managing conflict are the keys to living out your marriage vows. According to psychologists Howard Markman, Scott Stanley, and Susan L. Blumberg, it is not necessarily how much couples love each other that can best predict the future of their relationship but instead how they handle conflict and disagreement.[3]

Markman, Stanley, and Blumberg have carefully researched a sample of one hundred and fifty couples for thirteen years. They observed couples during their engagements and after their wedding days.[4] In their research, using only data collected from couples prior to marriage, they have been able to predict with eighty-two to ninety-three percent accuracy which couples will go on to be divorced and which will stay happily married.[5] This "means . . . for many couples, the seeds of [distress and future] divorce are [planted] prior to marriage."[6] A couple's premarital patterns of communication and conflict resolution may strongly predict divorce. The good news is that conflict management skills are most easily learned and readily produce change.

Since conflict management is highly predictive of divorce and most amenable to change, understanding and applying conflict management expertise is vital to the success of a marriage. Although some things are beyond our control, we can improve in this area. Thus, the challenge is to work hard and continually learn better ways to manage conflict with your (future) spouse.

Lord,

I pray for improved communication with my (future) spouse. May our words build up, speak truth, and articulate our thoughts, ideas, and opinions. In the process, build a bridge of understanding between us. Protect us from destructive words. Put an end to any conflict. More than anything, may we experience Your transformational work in our lives. Holy Spirit, please empower us to love with grace and kindness. This we pray, in Your holy name. Amen.

ONE

Pick a topic (one that is not controversial) to discuss with your (future) spouse for three to five minutes. At the conclusion of your talk, analyze your communication skills by answering the following questions.

NOTE: *Don't look at the questions until after the conversation.*

Quit cheating. Have you had the conversation? Then don't look at the questions!

Did one partner dominate the conversation?

Were questions asked in such a way as to draw out the other person's thoughts and opinions?

Did each of you make consistent eye contact? What did your body language communicate?

Was the other person actively listening or just waiting to talk next?

Did you speak directly and concisely or draw the conversation on verbosely?

Name several things you appreciate about your partner's communication skills.

TWO

Read and analyze the following Scriptures. Beside each write a simple principle to follow when communicating with your (future) spouse.

Proverbs 12:18

Proverbs 18:13

Luke 6:45

Ephesians 4:29

Colossians 3:12-15

James 1:19

THREE

Select an animal that best describes the way you, as an individual, handle conflict. Describe, in detail, why you chose that animal. Name some of the character qualities you share. What is positive about the way you handle conflict? What is negative? Discuss with one another.

Dealing with Conflict

On a scale of one to ten, how would you rate the level of conflict during your relationship thus far?

1   2   3   4   5   6   7   8   9   10

Do you believe the level of conflict in your relationship will increase or decrease after five years of marriage? Why or why not?

What is your natural response when dealing with conflict?

When conflict arises, you would like your partner to know that you really need these three things to happen:

1.

2.

3.

FOUR

Rate the following statements using this system:
A: Almost all of the time; S: Some of the time; N: Almost Never

___ When my feelings get hurt, I openly explain what is going on inside of me.

___ When I have a problem with someone, I immediately go to them and discuss it.

___ When discussing a problem, I feel my partner understands me.

___ I usually initiate our conversations.

___ My (future) spouse has tried to manipulate me or others with persuasive speech.

___ I use the "silent treatment" when I am mad or frustrated over an issue.

___ We have equal time to express our views when having a discussion.

___ I seem afraid to voice my point of view during a discussion.

___ I usually cry, yell, or get angry when we are fighting.

___ In order to end an argument, I give up discussing the issue.

___ I am comfortable expressing my love verbally to my (future) spouse.

___ Arguments between us end in a resolution.

Share your responses with your (future) spouse. Compare your answers with his or hers. Discuss your reasoning behind each answer.

List three specific ways you can improve your communication, listening, and conflict management skills.

DRIVING QUESTIONS

WHAT IS GOOD COMMUNICATION?
HOW CAN WE COMMUNICATE EFFECTIVELY?

How often do you sit down as a couple to simply talk with one another? Do you set time aside specifically for this purpose? Why or why not?

What do you need and expect from each other in terms of openness and depth of communication? How do your needs and expectations differ?

How would you deal with a breach in trust?

What in your communication style (e.g., behavior, tone of voice, choice of words, etc.) might interfere with your (future) spouse's understanding of what you are trying to say?

HOW WAS CONFLICT HANDLED IN YOUR HOME OF ORIGIN?

Was yelling and screaming a common occurrence in your home? Or was every effort made to avoid conflict and confrontation—even to the detriment of the family?

We all bring baggage into a marriage. Would your baggage fit into a tote bag, suitcase, or a crate? What steps have you taken to "unpack" your baggage?

Does conflict trigger certain emotions in you even today—insecurity, fear, anxiety, anger, etc.?

WHAT ARE THE HOT BUTTONS THAT YOUR PARTNER MOST OFTEN PUSHES?

What should you do if you and your (future) spouse come to a situation of conflict and feel strongly that the other person is at fault?

Do you think the level of conflict for most couples will increase or decrease after marriage? Why or why not?

WHAT IS YOUR TYPICAL PATTERN WHEN MANAGING CONFLICT?

There are four unhealthy patterns that are most common in dealing with conflict.[7] Identify the pattern(s) you tend to exhibit in conflict.

- **Escalation** *"occurs when partners respond back and forth negatively to each other, continually upping the ante so that conditions get worse and worse."[8]*
- **Invalidation** *occurs when "one partner subtly or directly puts down the thoughts, feelings, or character of the other."[9]*
- **Withdrawal** *or* **Avoidance** *occurs when "one partner shows an unwillingness to get into or stay with important discussions. "[10]*
- **Negative Interpretation** *occurs when a person interprets the motives of his or her (future) spouse much more negatively than that person intended.[11]*

What is your typical pattern when managing conflict?

What are you like when you are mad?

What are some positive ways to short-circuit unhealthy patterns of conflict?

SYNOPSIS

"Men and women have been miscommunicating—or not communicating at all—for thousands of years. And all too often, relationships break down because someone can't 'hear' what his or her spouse is trying to say. All too often, couples give up on a relationship that could have been a success."[12]

HOLLY HUDSON

When I (Carla) slip into my withdrawal pattern and Byron escalates, tensions rise and we completely miss the mark with one another. We have observed that the closest relationships have the highest risk for disappointment, hurt, and rejection. Because of this reality, an important part of good communication is a commitment to forgiveness and resolving conflict. The free exchange of thoughts, ideas, and opinions, engulfed with honesty, is also vital to meaningful communication—all the while, couples remaining totally committed to one another.

A FEW KEYS TO GOOD COMMUNICATION

As issues arise, we have a choice in how we will respond to these oftentimes painful experiences. My first instinct is to follow my emotional response that may be rooted in selfishness and pride. My second choice is a God-centered, supernatural response rooted in love. Jesus serves as our model.

Good communication requires transparency. For many couples, their families of origin did not model transparency in the home. Transparency and vulnerable communication can be difficult, especially for men. As Dr. James Dobson points out, "Research makes it clear that little girls are blessed with greater linguistic ability than little boys, and it remains a lifelong talent. Simply stated, [a wife] talks more than [a husband]. As an adult, she typically expresses her feelings and thoughts far better than her husband and is often irritated by his reticence. God may have given her [fifty thousand] words per day and her husband only [twenty-five thousand]. He comes home from work with 24,975 used up and merely grunts his way through the evening. He may descend into Monday night football while his wife is dying to expend her remaining [twenty-five thousand] words."[13]

God created marriage to be different from all other relationships—one in which we can truly be free to share the deepest parts of ourselves with our spouses. As you think of being transparent with your mate, remember that transparency begins with being open to God. This openness reduces our pride as we humbly trust ourselves to Him. God then gives us the ability to be open with others.

Good communication requires listening. For me to be present with Byron means that I must be prepared to temporarily be absent to myself. More often than not, people speak too much and listen too little—causing communication struggles. Good listening involves your undivided attention, sensitivity, and discernment. Good listening takes time.

"The pause button on my tongue's remote control should get much more use than the play button."[14]
GARY THOMAS

POWERFUL WORDS HEAL MARITAL HURTS.

Do not bury your hurt feelings, but lovingly confront your mate when you are hurt. Here are some helpful suggestions for confrontation:

- Speak the truth in love (Eph. 4:15).

- Attack the problem and not each other.

- Avoid confronting your mate in public or in front of your children.

Every day that you are married you will have a chance to build each other up or tear each other down. Your spouse is the greatest gift God has given you—your most prized possession. Use your words to pour courage into your mate. Listen as he or she talks to you. Keep in mind—this is one skill you can actually improve quickly. Remember, the area of communication requires constant attention.

As Byron and I have discovered, learning to communicate and manage conflict is crucial to living out the marriage covenant. This lifelong process will teach you more about yourself and God than you ever thought possible. Hang in there—it is worth the energy!

IN-LAWS
and FUTURE
INTENTIONS

WHERE ARE WE HEADED?

OVERVIEW

The purpose of this section is to help you navigate your homes of origin together as you define healthy patterns for your new marriage. As you evaluate the contents of this study, you will be challenged to think through, dream about, and pray for your future together as husband and wife.

> *"A journey is like marriage. The certain way to be wrong is to think you control it."[1]*
> **JOHN STEINBECK**

> ## "A MAN WILL LEAVE HIS FATHER AND MOTHER AND CLEAVE UNTO HIS WIFE."

"If you cannot get rid of the family skeleton,
you may as well make it dance."[2]
GEORGE BERNARD SHAW

These days, we have a tendency to move from one event to the next. Our lifestyles are not conducive to reflection or using personal mementos to remind us of particular experiences. The engagement period and first years of marriage are a good time of assessment. It's really easy to run past the wedding and into a new marriage without slowing down to evaluate life and provide intentional direction for the future.

When you marry, people say, you don't just marry your partner, you marry two families. Which is true. You're not just entering into a relationship with your spouse; you're entering into ongoing, lifelong relationships with your in-laws as well.

But it's also true that as you cleave to your mate, you are leaving your family of origin. When you marry, you create a new family of your own—a separate spiritual unit. It's the *two* that become one. Not the six. Not the eleven.

EXTENSIVE TRANSITION

For some of you, leaving your past family history and marrying into a fresh start is a very welcome change. However, if you fail to learn from your struggles and heal past hurts, it will be difficult to enter into a healthy marriage relationship. Every marriage will undoubtedly have struggles of its own. For others of you, leaving home will be the toughest part of getting married because you have a favorable family past with many rich traditions and warm memories.

"If you want to go quickly, go alone. If you want to go far, go together."[3]

AFRICAN PROVERB

Hopefully during these weeks of learning how "to have and to hold" one another in your new marriage, you have gained a few new skills and have encountered God in a real and personal way. To live intentionally, it is crucial to put into practice all that you are learning. Leaving and cleaving requires gaining a vision of where you are headed. Proverbs 29:18 (KJV) reminds us, "Where there is no vision the people perish."

Simply put, leaving and cleaving involves an extensive transition, and it is vital for you to reflect on the past while walking into the future.

O powerful God of today and tomorrow,
Please make our thoughts agreeable to Your will—thus our
plans will be established. Direct our steps and make them sure.
"For who hath known the mind of the Lord, that he may instruct
him? But we have the mind of Christ!" (1 Cor. 2:16, KJV). Allow
Your truth to set us free so that we don't speculate. Today is a
new day and we're not sure what lies ahead. Please know, we
commit our future and marriage to You. We are Yours. Today
belongs to You, not us. You are the potter, and we are the clay.
We desire for You to be our counselor and guide us through the
journey. Allow Your power to mark each step. Stop us if we are
headed in the wrong direction. Push us to move forward. If we
are selfish, bring us back to reality so we don't go our own way.
Please fill us with Your peace and Your power. In the name of
Jesus we pray. Amen.

PREP WORK

ONE

Family history is one of the most underestimated influences in marriage. Take a few minutes to reflect on your home of origin. How will your new marriage be influenced by your past experiences?

List three words that describe your relationship with your father. Your mother.

How have these two relationships shaped you?

How will you deal with conflict with your spouse's parents?

How will you respond if your parents give you money, possessions, and so forth?

How will you respond to his or her parents in working through major decisions?

List your top three favorite family traditions, gatherings, or celebrations. What would you like to carry forward in your new family?

Where will you spend your first Thanksgiving as a married couple? Christmas? How will you make that decision annually?

TWO

Read these insightful Scripture passages and write down your thoughts.

Genesis 2:23-24

Exodus 18:13-24

Amos 3:3

Matthew 6:33-34

Ephesians 6:1-3

THREE

Plan a fun date to talk through these "remember whens" and "what ifs."
- *Pull out the mementos of your relationship (old pictures, letters, cards, gifts, restaurant menus, stuffed animals, dried roses, etc.).*
- *Reminisce about the early days of your relationship.*
- *Talk about how you first met and what you thought of your (future) spouse the first time you interacted.*
- *Reflect on how much you have grown as a couple.*

What is the funniest thing that has happened during your dating days? Write it below so you can refer back to this Bible study book five to ten years from now.

Up to this point in life, what has been the most influential source of information about marriage for you? After you are married, how will you continue to learn?

What dreams do you have for your marriage? How are you going to pursue godly goals as you move forward toward a healthy, lasting relationship?

Do you feel free to think about doing new things or taking new risks? Do you allow your partner to think big? Do you dream even when finances or circumstances seem opposed to any possibility of fulfillment?

FOUR

MARRIAGE & FAMILY VISION

> "Where there is no vision, the people perish."
> **PROVERBS 29:18 (KJV)**

Reflect over what God has taught you during your engagement and this course. Attempt to develop a vision and plan as you move forward. Write simple statements defining what you want to do (goals) and how you will accomplish them (plan). Remember, your future intentions are not the end, just a means to that end. Look back at Matthew 6:33-34 before you begin.

AREA	FUTURE INTENTION (GOAL)	THE PLAN (HOW AND WHEN?)
MARRIAGE		
CAREER		
SPIRITUAL		
FINANCIAL		
FAMILY		
PERSONAL MINISTRY		
OTHER		

DRIVING QUESTIONS

HOW DO YOU CREATE A NEW FAMILY UNIT?

What is the purpose of your new marriage?

What kind of marriage partners do we want to be? How do we want to treat each other?

What kind of parents would we want to be? What principles would we want to teach our children to help them prepare for adulthood and to lead responsible, caring lives?

DOES HONORING PARENTS AND OBEYING THEM GO HAND IN HAND?

Is it okay for either of you to talk with parents about the problems in your marital relationship?

What expectations do you have for being together with your extended family? How much is too much connectedness for you?

What kind of support do you expect from your partner when his or her parents are putting pressure on you?

What can be learned from Exodus 20:12 and Ephesians 6:2-3?

How is honoring and respecting our parents obeying the Lord? Does this mean we must follow all of their advice? Why? Why not?

HOW DO VISION AND INTENTIONALITY PROVIDE MEANING FOR LIFE?

How is creating a family mission statement valuable to our future intentions?

How can we both support each other in our respective goals?

How do we want to give back?

How do we imagine our marriage ten years from now?

WHAT LEGACY WILL YOU LEAVE?

What do we want to be known for? What reputation do we want to have? What is the key theme you would want to hear at your funeral or the words you'd want etched on your tombstones?

What does success look like for our new family?

What do we want to pass on to the next generation? How will we go about doing this?

How can our marriage best represent the values we believe?

SYNOPSIS

MORE THAN MOVING OUT

"Leaving father and mother" involves far more than just moving out of the house. It means moving beyond full dependence upon them. This requires leaving a parent-centered life and a parent-controlled life where your emotions and decisions revolve around your parents. Note "two of the factors sociologists have identified as being highly significant to the success of a marriage [are:]

1. Whether people have emotionally separated from their parents in a healthy way, and

2. Whether [people] have had an opportunity to live on their own by themselves before they married.

If both of these conditions existed, they have a better opportunity for a successful marriage."[4]

HONOR THY FATHER AND MOTHER

Whether you have a close relationship with your parents now or not, work toward a healthy relationship by loving and honoring your parents. As we grow into adults, we increasingly realize that everyone, including our parents, has baggage. We all need grace and forgiveness.

It is important to avoid triangulation—when three parties are involved in a he said/she said disagreement and one says something about the other to a third party instead of going directly to the person. Couples should have a united front and allow the son or daughter to deal directly with his or her parent. The key is to show honor and respect. Open and honest communication is vital.

WHO GIVES THIS BRIDE AWAY?

The symbolism of the father giving the bride away at the altar provides a beautiful picture of what it means to leave and to cleave. In biblical times, a young man had to earn his right to marry the bride. Although both the groom's father and the bride's father determined the arrangement, it was not uncommon for a young man to be required to work for years to pay a dowry to compensate for the loss of a daughter's help to the family.

When I (Byron) gave our daughter away at the altar, I realized that it is a significant statement from the most important man in the bride's life to her new groom.

A father is, in effect, saying, "I've loved, provided, and protected my valued possession up until this point—now I am entrusting her to you. Take good care of her." Or in cases where a father is not present, family and friends stand with the bride and give her away, charging the new husband with the care and responsibility of the family unit being created—including the bride's spiritual, emotional, and physical well-being.

Certainly, families are still very important, but parents are no longer the key people in the bride and groom's life. At the altar and in life, parents must loosen their grip, relinquish control, and offer support as they give their blessing. Then, they should take a 50-yard-line seat to be the biggest fans.

THE JOURNEY AHEAD—CREATING A LEGACY

The couple is responsible to create a new path together all the while creating their own traditions, warm memories, and rich experiences. The framework you lay today will guide, stretch, and determine the direction of your marriage.

Remember, the first five years of marriage may either lay a foundation you can build on or they may cause you to spend the next five or ten years trying to dig out of the rubble.

During the engagement and marriage process it is vital to evaluate who you are, where you have come from, and what kind of support system you have in place.

As you meet at the altar, may your wedding day fulfill your dreams. More importantly, we challenge you to cooperate with God's Spirit in your life as you learn to love like He loves. As you journey down the trail, hang on! It is full of adventure, and the best part is that God faithfully works and provides in our lives (Phil. 1:6).

> "By wisdom a house is built, and through understanding
> it is established; through knowledge its rooms are
> filled with rare and beautiful treasures."
> **PROVERBS 24:3-4**

> "For the LORD gives wisdom, from his mouth
> come knowledge and understanding."
> **PROVERBS 2:6**

By the way, don't forget to enjoy the process. Have fun! The best is yet to come.

APPENDIX

PERSONAL BUDGET WORKSHEET

INCOME

TOTAL INCOME	
LESS TITHING (GIVING)	
LESS TAXES (ALL)	
LESS DEBT REPAYMENT	
LESS SAVING FOR LONG-TERM	
NET SPENDABLE INCOME	

EXPENSES

LOAN/NEW CAR SAVINGS	
AUTO-INSURANCE	
FUEL/OIL	
SERVICE	
STATE LICENSE AND TAX	
TOTAL AUTO	
BARBER/BEAUTY	
CASH	
CLOTHING	

EXPENSES

EDUCATION	
RECREATION AND ACTIVITY	
DINING OUT	
VACATIONS	
TOTAL ENTERTAINMENT	
GIFTS	
MEDICAL	
MISCELLANEOUS	
GROCERIES	
TOTAL MISCELLANEOUS	
RENT/MORTGAGE	
TELEPHONE	
UTILITIES	
ELECTRIC	
GAS	
WATER	
TOTAL HOUSING	
TOTAL EXPENSES	
MARGIN INCOME (Minus Expenses)	

NOTE: This assignment was adapted from Larry Burkett-Crown Financial Ministries and Dave Ramsey's material.
See "Find Help" at crown.org

PERCENTAGE GUIDE FOR FAMILY BUDGETING

MARRIED COUPLE

GROSS HOUSEHOLD INCOME	$15K	$25K	$35K	$45K	$55K	$65K	$115K
Tithe	10%	10%	10%	10%	10%	10%	10%
Taxes	6.4%	15.2%	19%	21.2%	22.5%	24.7%	30%
NET SPENDABLE INCOME	$12,540	$18,700	$24,850	$30,960	$37,125	$42,445	$69,000
Housing	40%	36%	32%	30%	30%	30%	29%
Food	15%	12%	13%	12%	11%	11%	11%
Auto	15%	12%	13%	14%	14%	13%	13%
Insurance	5%	5%	5%	5%	5%	5%	5%
Debts	5%	5%	5%	5%	5%	5%	5%

Net Spendable percentages above add to 100%.

Entertainment/ Recreation	3%	6%	6%	7%	7%	7%	8%
Clothing	4%	5%	5%	6%	6%	7%	7%
Savings	4%	5%	5%	5%	5%	5%	5%
Medical/ Dental	4%	4%	4%	4%	4%	4%	4%
Misc.	5%	5%	7%	7%	8%	8%	8%
Investments	5%	5%	5%	5%	5%	5%	5%

NOTE: This assignment was adapted from Larry Burkett-Crown Financial Ministries' material.

TOP TEN COMMONLY IDENTIFIED INTIMACY NEEDS

Look over this list of ten intimacy needs.[1] First, mark the three needs you consider the most important for you to receive from your partner right now. Next, mark the three needs you think your partner would consider most important to receive from you right now.

MYSELF	INTIMACY NEEDS	MY PARTNER
	Acceptance—deliberate and ready reception with a favorable positive response	
	Affection—to communicate care and closeness through physical touch	
	Appreciation—to communicate with words and feelings of personal gratefulness for another	
	Approval—expressed commendation; to think and speak well of	
	Attention—to take thought of another and convey appropriate interest and support; to enter into another's "world"	
	Comfort (empathy)—to come alongside with word, feeling and touch; to give consolation with tenderness	
	Encouragement—to urge forward and positively persuade toward a goal	
	Respect—to value and regard highly; to convey great worth	
	Security—confidence of harmony in relationships; free from harm	
	Support—come alongside and gently help carry a load	

HOW WE RELATE TO GOD

Adapted from Sacred Pathways by Gary Thomas

NATURALISTS: LOVING GOD OUT OF DOORS

"Naturalists...seek God by surrounding themselves with all that He has made. They would prefer to leave any building, however beautiful ... to pray to God beside a river [or a lake]."[2] Jesus loved to use creation as a tool to teach truths of God. An example can be found in the parable of the sower and seed in Matthew 13:2-23.

SENSATES: LOVING GOD WITH THE SENSES

"Sensate Christians want to be lost in the awe, beauty, and splendor of God. When these Christians worship, they want to be filled with sights, sounds and smells that overwhelm them."[3] The five senses are God's most effective inroad to their hearts. In the fourteenth chapter of Mark (vv. 3-9), we see a woman anointing Jesus with perfume. Because we know it was very expensive, the smell of the fragrance must have been beautiful!

TRADITIONALISTS: LOVING GOD THROUGH RITUAL AND SYMBOL

"Traditionalists are fed by what are often termed the historic dimensions of faith: rituals, symbols, sacraments, and sacrifice. These Christians tend to have a disciplined life of faith. ... Frequently they enjoy regular attendance at church, services, tithing, keeping the Sabbath, and so on. Traditionalists have a need for ritual and structure."[4] Jesus instituted the practice of the Lord's Supper himself as we see recorded in the fourteenth chapter of Mark's Gospel (vv. 12-26). He instructed his disciples (then and today) to follow his example and to "do this in remembrance of Me."

ASCETICS: LOVING GOD IN SOLITUDE AND SIMPLICITY

"Ascetics want nothing more than to be left alone in prayer. ... They are uncomfortable in any environment that keeps them from 'listening to the quiet.'"[5] "Very early in the morning, while it was still dark, Jesus got up, left the house and went off to a solitary place, where he prayed" (Mark 1:35).

ACTIVISTS: LOVING GOD THROUGH CONFRONTATION

"Activists serve a God of justice, and their favorite Scripture is often the account of Jesus cleansing the temple. They define *worship* as standing against evil and calling sinners to repentance. These Christians often view the church as a place to recharge their batteries so they can go back into the world to wage war against injustice."[6] A wonderful example in Scripture of loving God through confrontation can be found in the fourth chapter of Matthew when Jesus confronts Satan in the wilderness.

CAREGIVERS: LOVING GOD BY LOVING OTHERS

"Caregivers serve God by serving others. They often claim to see Christ in the poor and needy, and their faith is built up by interacting with other people. ... Whereas caring for others might wear many of us down, this recharges a caregiver's batteries."[7] Throughout Scripture, especially in the Gospels, we can see Jesus expressing His love for others by caring for their physical needs. In Matthew 8, we see Jesus healing the sick. In Mark 6, he feeds over 5,000 people. And in Luke 6, he even speaks of loving one's enemies. However, his ultimate act of love can be found in his death on the cross.

ENTHUSIASTS: LOVING GOD WITH MYSTERY AND CELEBRATION

"Excitement and mystery in worship [are] the spiritual lifeblood of enthusiasts. These Christians are enthusiastic motivators for God and the Christian life. ... They don't just want to know concepts, but to experience them, to feel them, to be moved by them."[8] One place in Scripture where there can be found both celebration of God and yet an underlying mysterious awe is definitely in the telling of Jesus' birth. Matthew, Mark and Luke both describe this time as joyful and mysterious, for even Mary, his own mother, did not know what was to come.

CONTEMPLATIVES: LOVING GOD THROUGH ADORATION

"The contemplative seeks to know the personhood of God and to be caught up in pursuing a loving experience with God. "Contemplatives refer to God as their lover, and images of a loving Father and Bridegroom predominate their view of God. ... These Christians seek to love God with the purest, deepest and brightest love imaginable."[9] We see in the account of Luke (10:38-42) where Jesus commends Mary of Bethany as she sat and worshipped at his feet, simply by "being still and knowing" Him (Ps. 46:10).

INTELLECTUALS: LOVING GOD WITH THE MIND

"Intellectuals might be skeptics or committed believers, but in either case they are likely to be studying. ... These Christians live in the world of concepts. They may feel closest to God when they first understand something new about him. 'Faith' is something to be understood as much as experienced."[10] Luke gives us the best example of loving God with the mind in chapter two, where Jesus, as a young boy, is found "in the temple courts, sitting among the teachers, listening to them and asking them questions" (v. 46).

SEXUAL INTIMACY Q&A

In our years of marriage preparation, we've found couples have many questions regarding sexual intimacy, but they are often afraid to ask. Below, we've compiled a list. While this list is not exhaustive, we hope you find it helpful.

Introduction

1. Do most young, (to-be-married) married men have a false perception that they are going to spend the majority of their day having sex?
Yes. In our culture, we are infiltrated with sex, and those messages are often geared toward men. We should work to redeem our views of sexuality from the worldly distortions we so often see. Instead, we must align our perspectives on sexuality with the way that God created it—as a gift from Him.

2. Why do many Christian women deny their sexual desires or have trouble giving themselves permission to celebrate the sensuous pleasures of married love or?
Although most Christian women believe sex is a gift from God, in their minds the words godly and sensuous do not go together, especially in our culture. Many women feel that they have to disassociate themselves from anything erotic or sensuous in order to be godly. It is very rare for couples to enter marriage without some sort of baggage from past hurts or confusing messages. It's really important for women to know that when God created them He integrated their sexuality with their spirituality. A look into the Song of Solomon shows a wife who is both sensuous and uninhibited. Christian marriages have the ability to infuse the physical and the deep soul stirring of the spiritual.

3. What is wrong with referring to sex as "getting some" or "doing it" (or other terms)?
Sex is not "getting some" because this implies that sex is like a material possession. If it's "doing it" then sex becomes a performance trap of how well you acted. It's an activity judged by your performance and your performance alone. These terms are not appropriate because they do not take into account the deep, spiritual connection that you and your spouse maintain. God has brought you together as one. Along with that oneness, you are to care for, honor, and respect your spouse as yourself. Our perspectives and speech regarding sexual intimacy should always reflect a heart of love and consideration. We have to change our mind-set and really consider others as more important than ourselves.

4. Can our sex lives teach us valuable spiritual lessons?
Yes, our sex lives can teach us critical lessons about our spiritual lives. First Thessalonians 4 clearly states that it is God's will for us to be sanctified or made more like Christ, and then very quickly it brings in the sexual. The passage explains how we should avoid sexual immorality and learn to control our own bodies in a way that is both holy and honorable. Consider that sanctification and sex are discussed in the same passage. We are convinced that God uses the marriage relationship to teach us how to love as Christ loved.

5. How can couples gain more freedom in their sexuality?
Identify distortions and replace the cultural lies that you have believed about sex with God's view of sex. These distorted thoughts are frequently born out of a human's twisted view of physical intimacy—a view which often involves premarital, extramarital, or perverted relationships as a means to only fulfill a self-centered physical desire. The distortion can also come from cultural Christianity that miscommunicates the sinful side of human sexuality. Sometimes it's easier to declare all of human sexuality as wrong and bad rather than deal with it honestly. Jesus directly addresses the marriage relationship as a one flesh union, referring to marital intimacy and the sensual, sexual way He created us.

6. The author of Hebrews talks about keeping the marriage bed honorable and the bed undefiled. What exactly did he mean by this?
In Hebrews 13:4, the Greek meaning of the English word *bed* refers to "cohabitation by a married man and a woman with obvious more specific implications of sexual intercourse."[11] In addition, the meaning of the word *undefiled* in Greek is "pure, spotless, and unblemished."[12]

7. How would you describe a godly physical relationship?
According to God's design, physical intimacy for a married couple should be exciting, fulfilling, and enjoyable. This part of the relationship should be seen as intrinsically good and pure. It is a precious gift that you can share with your spouse for the rest of your lives. It allows you to grow in intimacy with the individual with whom you will be sharing the rest of your life.

My Wedding Night & Beyond (Honeymoon Expectations)

1. What anticipations or concerns do you have regarding the first night?
Take some of the pressure off of the first night, and let yourselves relax, laugh, and enjoy being married. Talk through your expectations. What do you picture as the perfect first night? Communicate honestly with one another and be kind. As with any part of your relationship, you'll grow more comfortable with sexual intimacy in time.

2. What if you've had sex before, how do you deal with the fact that this is not your first time?
If you have had sex before, you must be honest enough with yourselves to confess that you have pursued self and not God in the area of sex. God wants us to get real, admit our selfish behavior, acknowledge its destructive nature and agree that God's way is best. If we confess, repent, and strive to obey God, He will help us walk in His ways. That's why we need a Savior.

3. If a couple has already had sex together, what is so special about their wedding night?
The book *A Celebration of Sex for Newlyweds* recounts a pastor's advice, "Just because [a couple has] already had sex, don't let them treat their wedding night in an ordinary way. This is their first time of truly making love. Let them build on their new covenant as they discover exciting and deeper levels of sexual intimacy." [13]

4. Will sex be painful the first time for a woman who is a virgin?
Statistics tell us in the first sexual encounter fifty percent of women experience some pain, twenty percent no pain, and thirty percent experience severe pain.[14] For many women, some of this pain could certainly have been lessened. It's important for the female to be physically ready for intercourse. Otherwise, she may not be adequately lubricated or dilated, and the man may move too quickly.

5. Why is orgasm so easy for a male?
Research shows that for an average man to have an orgasm, it takes three to five minutes of direct or indirect stimulation.[15] For an average female, it will take fifteen to forty minutes to reach orgasm—and that's once the female mind and emotion have warmed up and communicated with the physical.[16] Men need to understand that women desire sex but move at a different pace than men do—and that's part of God's good design.

Practice Makes Perfect (The Act of Sex)

1. Why is it necessary and helpful to discuss the act of sexual intimacy?
Unfortunately, the myths and miscommunications of our culture have clouded most people's perspectives on sex. We hope these discussions about sexual intimacy will help couples get off to a healthy start and avoid some of the potential frustrating pitfalls. Knowledge and practice lead to the ultimate goal of pleasing one another.

2. How can you discover what pleases your spouse the most?
Both partners should communicate and gently guide the other to demonstrate how to bring the most pleasure. Communication is the only way that your spouse will know what pleases you the most. Great lovemaking must be interactive and flow from your heart. There's a great deal of difference between having sex and making love.

3. Can you explain the experience of vulnerability and intimacy between husband and wife?
Christian sex therapist Christopher McCluskey has created a helpful model, the "Lovemaking Cycle," to describe the experience of vulnerability and intimacy between husband and wife. He emphasizes that if one part of the cycle is neglected, lovemaking will become clunky. Keep in mind—this is not designed to be a formula or an easy four-step process. It's designed to help us gain knowledge. The Lovemaking Cycle is:

1. *Atmosphere,*
2. *Arousal,*
3. *Apex,*
4. *Afterglow.*

Much like a spiral, one area escalates into the next until completion.[17]

4. What does Scripture say about oral sex?
In regards to oral sex, Scripture is pretty silent. The basic principle is that you should never make your mate feel guilty or inhibited because he or she does not feel comfortable with a given behavior. Both of you should feel completely okay before moving forward with any sexual practice that the Bible is silent about.

If Only I Knew (Bedroom Etiquette)

1. Is it important for what happens in the bedroom stay in the bedroom?
Sit down together and discuss your expectations for privacy. We encourage you to maintain privacy. Making your sex life private will build and grow a deeper level of trust.

2. Does it hurt to have sex?
It is God's design for a husband to pleasure his wife. The act itself can and should be pleasurable for both. For some women, though, the actual act of intercourse may be somewhat uncomfortable at different times in marriage. You may try some different things, including a variety of sexual positions or lubricants, to be more comfortable. Certainly severe pain is not normal. If you are experiencing severe pain, we recommend consulting your doctor.

3. Is there anything else to consider when thinking about proper sex etiquette in the bedroom?

1. Keep a sense of humor—sex will be funny and full of mishaps. That's okay.

2. Become uninhibited—let yourself go and enjoy the gift God's given you. Don't focus on the mess of it all.

3. Remain flexible—learn to go with the flow and be able to adapt easily.

4. Attempt to communicate—no topic should be off-limits.

5. Learn to extend grace—allow each other to make mistakes. That's how we learn best.

6. And lastly, be respectful—remember to break the barrier of being naked and not ashamed very, very respectfully.

Questions No One Wants to Talk About

1. Many men and women have had multiple sex partners. How can they make sure they do not have a sexually transmitted disease entering into the marriage relationship?

Many sexually transmitted diseases can be found through medical testing. The details of these tests and their implications should always be addressed by your physician.

2. My future spouse and I are presently having sex. We have been having sex prior to our engagement. Is this a big deal? What should we do?

It's critical to understand that sex is preserved for the marriage union. God created us to have sex within marriage when we become one. Often people will say, 'well we're going to get married,' and then have premarital sex. The fact is—you're not married. Abstaining from sex allows us to learn valuable lessons of self-control. So, whether, it's three weeks or three months, exert some discipline and allow God to teach you some incredible lessons in self-control.

3. Is it wrong to masturbate and does it cause problems in marriage?

This question is frequently debated in Christian circles. Masturbation is not directly addressed in Scripture, so it's probably not appropriate to be dogmatic from either viewpoint. We believe that masturbation is not healthy or appropriate for either the married or unmarried person. The greatest danger in masturbation stems from a person fantasizing or focusing on an image that is unrealistic in nature. Unrealistic expectations seem to miss the mark and leave a personal unsatisfied. Masturbation can bring emotional and mental baggage into the marriage. Sometimes the emotional and physical side effects can be destructive. Habits are hard to break, but it's important to learn how to practice restraint with your body. 1 Thessalonians 4:4 says, "Each of you should learn to control your own body in a way that is holy and honorable."

4. How far is "too far" when you are engaged?

If you're asking this question, you have probably crossed the line. Unfortunately, the Bible does not directly map out what we can and can't do physically during engagement. However, God desires for us to demonstrate self-control. Your physical body does not know the difference between being married or not. But the emotional, psychological, and especially the spiritual parts of you know the huge difference. The physical is only a representation of what is really going on inside emotionally and spiritually in both people. Throughout the Bible, it warns us not to be sexually immoral. It seems like God uses our human sexuality to help us learn valuable lessons of self-control. This self-control comes from a power beyond our natural selves. It comes from a supernatural God. We are convinced that He wants us to have a secure marriage relationship where passionate and uninhibited sex can take place.

5. Is it possible to get beyond the pain of sexual abuse?

Yes, absolutely. In fact, God's desire in His gracious healing process is to redeem those past hurts. This will take much more than human wisdom. It will take divine healing. God intends for you to be in a safe, secure relationship with your spouse and experience true intimacy. This requires trust. We are so sorry that your trust has been violated by another person. But make no mistake about it, Satan would love to keep you tied up in bondage with this issue. But Jesus Christ wants you to know the truth and allow the truth to set you free. You may feel dirty, but God has given you a clean and worthwhile life. We encourage you to talk with a trusted counselor about your feelings on this issue.

6. Should I be afraid of my future spouse having an affair?

Yes and no. Yes, "be careful that you don't fall" (1 Cor. 10:12). No couple is exempt from the fantasy and fraud of another person. It is important to work at maintaining the compatibility your relationship has been founded on. This requires consistent sexual relations and consistent communication.

ENDNOTES

INTRODUCTION

1. C. Silvester Horne, *David Livingstone: Mane of Prayer and Action* (Arlington Heights, IL: Christian Liberty Press, 1999).

2. Toneal M. Jackson, *Pleasing Your Partner: A Spiritual Guide to Happiness* (Bloomington, IN: AuthorHouse ™, 2010).

SESSION 1

1. Stephen M. Crotts; "The Ties that Bind" *Carolina Study Center* accessed on 3/15/17. Available online at *carolinastudycenter.com/the-ties-that-bind*.

2. James Strong, *Strong's Exhaustive Concordance of the Bible*, accessed on March 13, 2017, via Bible Hub. Available online at *biblehub.com/hebrew/1285.htm*.

3. Jason D. Scott, *The Strength to Walk Away* (McKinney, TX: Integrity Oasis Publishing, LLC, 2016).

4. H. Norman Wright, *The Secrets of a Lasting Marriage* (Ventura, CA: Gospel Light, 1995), accessed via *mywsb.com*.

5. Tony Evans, *Marriage Matters* (Chicago: Moody Publishers, 2010).

6. David Egner, *What is the promise of marriage?* (Grand Rapids: RBC Ministries, 1992), 6.

SESSION 2

1. H. Norman Wright, *Starting Out Together: A Devotional for Dating or Engaged Couples* (Bloomington, Minnesota: Bethany House Publishers, 1996).

2. James Strong, *Strong's Exhaustive Concordance of the Bible*, accessed on March 15, 2017, via Blue Letter Bible.

Available online at *blueletterbible.org/lang/lexicon/lexicon.cfm?strongs=G2776*.

3. James Strong, *Strong's Exhaustive Concordance of the Bible*, accessed on March 15, 2017, via Bible Hub. Available online at *biblehub.com/greek/2776.htm*.

4. Matthew George Easton, *Easton's Illustrated Bible Dictionary* (New York: Cosimos, Inc., 2005), accessed via *mywsb.com*.

5. James Strong, *Strong's Exhaustive Concordance of the Bible*, accessed on March 15, 2017, via Blue Letter Bible. Available online at *blueletterbible.org/lang/lexicon/lexicon.cfm?Strongs=H5828&t=KJV*.

6. James Strong, *Strong's Exhaustive Concordance of the Bible* accessed on March 15, 2017, via Blue Letter Bible. Available online at *blueletterbible.org/lang/lexicon/lexicon.cfm?Strongs=H5048&t=KJV*.

7. James Strong, *Strong's Exhaustive Concordance of the Bible* accessed on March 15, 2017, via Blue Letter Bible. Available online at *blueletterbible.org/lang/lexicon/lexicon.cfm?strongs=H5046&t=KJV*.

8. Gary L. Thomas, *Sacred Influence: How God Uses Wives to Shape the Souls of Their Husbands* (Grand Rapids: Zondervan, 2006).

SESSION 3

1. Dave Ramsey, *The Total Money Makeover: Proven Plan for Financial Fitness* (Nashville: Thomas Nelson, 2003), 30.

2. Ron Blue, *Master Your Money: A Step-by-Step Plan for Experiencing Financial Contentment* (Chicago: Moody Publishers, 1986).

3. Erin El Issa, "2016 American Household Credit Card Debt Study" *Nerdwallet blog* Accessed on March 15, 2017.

Available online at *nerdwallet.com/blog/average-credit-card-debt-household/*.

4. Kate Gibson, "Who lives paycheck-to-paycheck? You might be surprised." *CBS News Moneywatch* August 11, 2016, accessed on March 15, 2017. Available online at *cbsnews.com/news/who-lives-paycheck-to-paycheck-you-might-be-surprised/*.

5. Lisa L. Payne, Kim Olver, and Deborah Roth, "The 10 Most Common Reasons People Get Divorced" *The Huffington Post Blog* September 16, 2015, accessed on March 17, 2017. Available online at *huffingtonpost.com/yourtango/10-most-common-reasons-people-divorce_b_8086312.html*.

6. Crown Financial, "The Financial Message of the Ministry" *Crown.org* January 25, 2012, accessed on March 15, 2017. Available online at *crown.org/Articles/tabid/107/entryid/83/Default.aspx*.

SESSION 4

1. Jill Savage, "Seven Ways to Develop Emotional Intimacy in Your Marriage" *Crosswalk.com* December 10, 2010, accessed on March 14, 2017. Available online at *crosswalk.com/family/marriage/seven-ways-to-develop-emotional-intimacy-in-your-marriage-11642928.html*.

2. Gary Thomas, "How to build a lifelong love: an interview with Gary Thomas" *Focus on the Family Canada* 2016, accessed on March 15, 2017. Available online at *focusonthefamily.ca/marriage/communication/how-to-build-a-lifelong-love-an-interview-with-gary-thomas*.

3. Gordon Edlin, Eric Golanty, Kelli McCormack Brown, *Essentials for Health and Wellness* (Sudbury, MA: Jones and Bartlett Publishers, 1997), 33.

4. David Hawkins, "Sexual Intimacy Begins with the Heart" Crosswalk.com June 21, 2011 accessed on May 3, 2017. Available online at *crosswalk.com/family/marriage/doctor-david/sexual-intimacy-begins-with-the-heart-11628157.html*.

SESSION 5

1. Charles R. Swindoll, *Getting Through the Tough Stuff* (Nashville: Thomas Nelson, 2004), 89-90.

2. Justin Taylor, "Lewis on Love and God." *The Gospel Coalition blog* July 15, 2010, accessed March 15, 2017. Available online at *blogs.thegospelcoalition.org/justintaylor/2010/07/15/lewis-on-love-and-god/*.

3. Jon M. Sweeney, *Francis of Assisi in His Own Words: The Essential Writings* (Brewster, MA: Paraclete Press, 2013), 16.

4. Adapted from Dennis and Barbara Rainey, *Building Your Mate's Self-Esteem* (Nashville: Thomas Nelson, Inc., 1995).

5. "Definition of busyness" *Merriam-Webster's Dictionary* Accessed May 2, 2017. Available online via merriam-webster.com/dictionary/busy.

SESSION 6

1. Robert Byrne, *The 2,548 Wittiest Things Anybody Ever Said* (New York: Touchstone, 2012).

2. Ed Wheat and Gaye Wheat, *Intended for Pleasure* (Grand Rapids: Revell, 1977), 215-216.

3. Katherine M. Hertlein, Gerald R. Weeks, Nancy Gambescia, eds., *Systematic Sex Therapy, Second Edition* (New York: Routledge, 2015), 55.

SESSION 7

1. Kevin Van Anglen, *Simplify, Simplify: And Other Quotations from Henry David Thoreau* (New York: Columbia University Press: 1996), 179.

2. Cathy A. Costantino and Christina Sickles Merchant, *Designing Conflict Management Systems: A Guide to Creating Productive and Healthy Organizations* (San Francisco: Jossey-Bass, 1996), xiii.

3. Howard J. Markman, Scott M. Stanley, and Susan L. Blumberg, *Fighting For Your Marriage* (San Francisco: John Wiley & Sons, Inc, 2010), 5.

4. Howard J. Markman, Scott M. Stanley, and Susan L. Blumberg, *Fighting For Your Marriage* (San Francisco: John Wiley & Sons, Inc, 1995), 4.

5. Ibid, Markman, Stanley Blumberg, 1995, 5.

6. Ibid, Markman, Stanley Blumberg, 2010, 12.

7. Ibid, Markman, Stanley Blumberg, 2010, 37.

8. Ibid, Markman, Stanley Blumberg, 2010, 42.

9. Ibid, Markman, Stanley Blumberg, 2010, 47.

10. Ibid, Markman, Stanley Blumberg, 2010, 57.

11. Ibid, Markman, Stanley Blumberg, 2010, 50.

12. Holly Hudson, "We Need to Talk" blog *Focus on the Family Africa blog* May 26, 2015, accessed on March 15, 2017. Available online at *safamily.co.za/we_need_to_talk*.

13. Dr. James Dobson, "Fundamentals of a Christian Marriage" *Dr. James Dobson's Family Talk™* accessed on March 15, 2017. Available online at *drjamesdobson.org/articles/pray-for-america/fundamentals-christian-marriage*.

14. Gary L. Thomas, *Sacred Marriage Gift Edition: Discover Your Soul's Path to God* (Grand Rapids: Zondervan, 2011), 48.

SESSION 8

1. John Steinbeck, *Travels with Charley: In Search of America* (New York: Penguin Books, 1962), 4.

2. Amanda Green, "14 of George Bernard Shaw's Most Brilliant Quotes." *Mental Floss* November 2, 2014, accessed on March 15, 2017. Available online at *mentalfloss.com/article/59813/14-george-bernard-shaws-most-brilliant-quotes*.

3. Maria Damanaki, "If you Want to Go Quickly, Go Alone. If You Want to Go Far, Go Together." *The Huffington Post blog* March 1, 2016, accessed on March 15, 2017. Available online at *huffingtonpost.com/maria-damanaki/if-you-want-to-go-quickly_b_9352480.html*.

4. H. Norman Wright, *Mothers, Sons and Wives* (Ventura, CA: Regal Books, 1994) Accessed on May 2, 2017 via *mywsb.com*.

APPENDIX

1. Ibid, Ferguson, 10.

2. Gary Thomas, *Sacred Pathways* (Grand Rapids: Zondervan, 1996).

3. Ibid.

4. Ibid.

5. Ibid.

6. Ibid.

7. Ibid.

8. Ibid.

9. Ibid.

10. Ibid.

11. James Strong, *Strong's Exhaustive Concordance of the Bible* accessed on April 3, 2017, via Blue Letter Bible. Available online at *blueletterbible.org/lang/lexicon/lexicon.cfm?Strongs=G2845&t=KJV*.

12. James Strong, *Strong's Exhaustive Concordance of the Bible* accessed on April 3, 2017, via Blue Letter Bible. Available online at *blueletterbible.org/lang/lexicon/lexicon.cfm?Strongs=G283&t=KJV*.

13. Douglas E. Rosenau, *A Celebration of Sex for Newlyweds* (Nashville: Thomas Nelson, 2002) 120-121.

14. Ed Wheat and Gloria Okes Perkins, *The First Years of Forever* (Grand Rapids: Zondervan, 1988), 95.

15. Dr. Mehmet Oz, MD, "Q&A Achieving Orgasm" *ShareCare* Accessed on March 15, 2017. Available online at *sharecare.com/health/achieving-orgasm/how-long-to-orgasm.*

16. Debby Herbenick, Ph.D., "10 Lessons About the Female Orgasm" *Men's Health*, April 27, 2015, accessed on March 15, 2017. Available online at *menshealth.com/10-lessons-about-female-orgasm.*

17. Christopher McCluskey and Rachel McCluskey, *When Two Become One: Enhancing Sexual Intimacy in Marriage* (Grand Rapids, Fleming H. Revell, 2004), 9, 82.

NOTES

NOTES

NOTES

NOTES

NOTES

What's Next?

ESSENTIAL STUDIES FOR MARRIED COUPLES

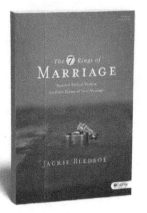

THE 7 RINGS OF MARRIAGE
Jackie Bledsoe
8 Sessions

From the engagement ring to years after the wedding ring, every season of a marriage requires renewed commitment, fresh perspective, and practical biblical wisdom. Each of the 7 "rings" outlined in this study will teach couples to view their marriage with the end in mind, ultimately leading to a lasting and fulfilling relationship. The 7 Rings include: the Engagement RING (the beginning), the Wedding RING (the commitment), DiscoveRING (the real you), PerseveRING (the work), RestoRING (the fixing), ProspeRING (the goal), and MentoRING (the payback).

Bible Study Book   005753519 $12.99
Leader Kit   005644102 $79.99

LifeWay.com/7Rings

A BEAUTIFUL DESIGN
Matt Chandler
9 Sessions

God created us to function according to His perfect design, and for all of human history, our world has been male and female. But our ever-changing culture faces challenges due to sin. More than ever the church needs to be a safe refuge for the gender confused, the sexually broken, the single, the married, and the divorced. In this study, Matt Chandler gives evidence that God's plan for man and woman is the ultimate design. And life lived within this beautiful and unchanging design leads to our greatest joy.

Bible Study Book 005782093 $12.99
Leader Kit   005782094 $99.99

LifeWay.com/BeautifulDesign